MW01146939

Beauty and the Bitch: Grace for the Worst in Me

Copyright © 2013 by Jan Meyers Proett

Cover art to the electronic edition copyright © 2013 by Bondfire Books, LLC.

See full line of Bondfire Books titles at www.bondfirebooks.com.

Electronic edition published 2013 by Bondfire Books LLC, Colorado. ISBN 9781629218366

Praise for *Beauty and the Bitch*

Jan's words will heal and minister life to the broken places for so many women. Instead of resorting to armor or performance, Jan encourages us to embrace the dignity and identity found in Christ. It's an honest and timely book for many women.

— Sarah Bessey, blogger and author of *Jesus Feminist*

The title of this book obviously grabbed my attention. But I'm so grateful I didn't stop with the cover, for what oozes from the chapters and paragraphs and lines and words is very good news, and heaven knows we need more of that. Author Jan Meyers Proett practices midwifery here. By confessionally sharing the pangs of her own story, Jan encourages the birth of something in you and me: *beauty*- not as the world defines but as God desires. This process is not pretty, but the world doesn't need more pretty. The world needs more beautiful. Thank you, Jan.

— John Blase, author of *Know When To Hold 'Em*

Every failure of love, cruel word, broken loyalty, withdrawal of care arises from the war within. We live out the war of our divided self and the debris casts a shadow over every relationship. Jan Meyers Proett has lovingly and graciously allowed us to enter her world to see not only the harm, but also the hope. The more we tell the truth about our war, the more healing our heart is open to receive. And the hope is always the beauty we have been made to be in the light of the true beauty of Jesus. *Beauty and the Bitch* pushes the envelope of language and invites us to consider the depths of what inflicts not only a woman's heart, but a man's as well. I wince at the B-word and how it may be used by a man against a woman or by a woman with cavalier contempt. Jan is a courageous woman to name her inner war with that word, but it is never the prerogative of any man, ever, no matter the depths of sin, to use that word against his wife or any other woman. May your reading invite you to the face of beauty you are and the one you are to become.

— Dan B. Allender, Ph.D., Professor of Counseling Psychology and Founding President, The Seattle School of Theology and Psychology

FOREWORD by STASI ELDREDGE

I forgot who I was.

Then I read Jan's book—and remembered.

Not that I read it all in one sitting, mind you. That would not be wise. Enjoying a feast at a four-star buffet takes lingering time. Saturating my heart in the truths I was invited to partake of in *Beauty and the Bitch* deserved at least as long. My heart is now filled with the memory of who I truly am.

I'm fortunate—I can keep coming back for more. And I will. There is life in her words. Light and life. Fearless truth. Vulnerable honesty. Soaring hope. Fiery love. The kind that changes us in the way we long to be changed. I have been seen and not rejected, but understood. Not only have I been understood, but I've been invited to see myself, my life, my way through the eyes of Love.

Don't let the title throw you. Though if you're reading this then you are at the very least *intrigued* and quite possibly have recognized yourself in the title. I sure did. And Jan? Well, Jan knows that of which she speaks. She is well read, well versed and well acquainted with all "B" words. Bravery. Battle. Bitch. And most deeply, with Beauty.

Beauty. Isn't it one of the richest of words? I say it out loud now and it settles on my tongue like a longed-for promise. Oh, how I want that to be the truest thing about me. Don't you? And are you like me, knowing that "beauty" is not what people experience through me as often as I'd like? Honestly, no one knows our messiness or our bitchiness better than we do ourselves. (Though we'd like to pretend others somehow miss it.)

The invitation extended in *Beauty and the Bitch* is to not turn our face away from ourselves but to take a fearless look. A grace-filled look. A look that we are safe to take because we do it while securely held in the embrace of our loving God who has already shamelessly, flagrantly decreed that we are beautiful. God says that beauty isn't just what we hope for but what is most deeply true of us. Already! Since Jesus—who sees so clearly—absolutely refuses to turn his face away from us, we are safe to embrace ourselves, too.

And though the idea to do so may be terrifying, and is certainly risky, it can be done. We can do it. I'm doing it. Jan is doing it. There is healing to be found there. In this stunning work, Jan shares intimately her journey, her failings, her pain, her *story*—and the steady restoring presence of Love throughout. It is overflowing with wisdom and hope; winsomely, brilliantly and honestly written. Read it. Take the risk. Choose to come more alive. Awaken. Come out of hiding and be found by the One who has always been pursuing you.

You are the Beauty. Yes, okay, sometimes you are the bitch, too. But because of the transforming presence and heroic invasion of the King of your heart, the bitch is not your destiny. *The beauty is.* The beauty is. If you will say yes to her. Say yes to

Jesus. Say yes to Love. Really, it's the only choice worth making.

Stasi Eldredge
Author of *Becoming Myself* and co-author of *Captivating*

Table of Contents

Chapter One
When Beauty Meets Bitch

The Ugly and the Glory

I threw a mug.

I'm not proud of it, but I did. It was my *momentum veritatis*, and the coffee splattered on the wall was witness to my foolishness.

And Steve was witness, of course. He was both witness and object of this meanness. Neither one of us could tell you what it was that started the argument (yes, it was one of *those*), but it escalated, as arguments do, and as it did, my blood turned cold, and my words turned biting.

Steve was full participant in the argument, no question, and he would tell you he had been getting smug. But what rose up in me in response was, well, awful. Somewhere in the mix, my face became red, my heart braced, and contemptuous mockery started flowing from my mouth. I cannot tell you the exact words that flew like missiles to my husband's heart, but they were cutting, sarcastic, and cruel, of the *What were you thinking?* and the *I could have told you would fail me* variety.

Momentarily, I heard myself and flooded with immense shame, which exploded in a crescendo of furious energy. I hurled the green-glazed pottery mug across the dining room, where it broke against the wall. I looked up and saw in Steve's eyes something that, truly, I would never want to see. His eyes held not anger, but bewildered disappointment. He was in disbelief. It killed me to see it.

This was not the woman he married. I was not the woman I am. I was an absolute bitch.

Now, some of you may be thinking, "Umm… throwing a mug is not good, but it is not *that* bad," and others of you are rightfully aghast. We all have different ideas of what qualifies us to be considered a "bitch." But I hope you can hear that it wasn't just the cup; it wasn't just that my behavior was bad. The energy in my heart was foul. My spirit was not only devoid of love, but was fueled with a desire to tear down and to harm.

I could call it childish, I suppose, but that is too anemic. I could say I was "wound up" or that I lost my temper, or I could find myriad other ways to tone down the foolishness of it, like we do when we want to hide. But the fact remains: all through that day, through a long series of exchanges with Steve, I had been picking, prodding, complaining. And bitch upon bitch hours in a day cascades into class five rapids of bad.

Thankfully, Steve remembers who I am. I don't want to tread on that, of course, but there is a hush that comes over me—a quiet hallelujah—each time I see myself through his eyes. He meets my controlling nature with strength, while still remembering who I really am. Life with Jan includes crazy mug moments alongside moments when he feels the deep respect I give him, and a whole lot of good loving. He says he loves the lighthearted but intentional nature God has crafted in me. He says he watches with delight as people come to drink of the beauty Jesus has grown in me. And he loves the open, vulnerable, caring heart I bring him. When he tells me all this, we delight together. I blush a bit, but I can—actually I *must*—enjoy those moments when beauty shows up because we both know how my loveliness can disintegrate, even with the raising of an eyebrow.

I know I am not alone in disintegrating into something less than lovely. This morning I slumped into the deep peace of being curled up near and cloistered with him. It was so still. The hush of breathing in, breathing out together in a cadence of spirit communion draped over me like a light blanket. I found music quietly, involuntarily beginning to stir within me. I hummed through a favorite song, then circled round again with a bit more confidence, and sang, reclining in Steve's arms. I wanted to sing over him, over us. I wanted to express the awe which only music begins to capture. I don't know how this may sound to you, but I found the sound of my own voice sweet, almost as if it matched my spirit. I felt beautiful. I was beautiful. And it was so nice to catch myself in such a state of being.

Sadly, it is not always so.

The title of this book mocks the reality, but we know it all too well: a predatory, animalistic, violent, crazed beast of a bitch lurks within the brambles of our hearts as women. We are not always beautiful. So

oh, when we are, all heaven and earth collide to say
Amen. And we intrinsically know that the *Amen*
cannot be forced. We grow weary of trying to either
"manage the beast"—trying to make her good—or
trying to repeat mantras of truth to ourselves to make
her go away. It doesn't work. Something else must
wash over our beast, calming her and eventually
replacing her. Unless a woman's beauty—the very life
of God within her—rises, then the beast will rise and
cause her to feel like there is no beauty in her at all.

It's okay to admit that you are a bitch, but it's also
crucial to see that there is beauty in you that wants to
come out—will come out. That's the wonderful
surprise: the life of God will always rise.

There is a quality to a woman's beauty that is
simply unmanageable. We can't produce it ourselves,
but we can make our hearts a welcome, responsive
place for beauty to live. Alexandr Solzhenitsyn said
that "if the too obvious, too straight branches of
Truth and Good are crushed or amputated and
cannot reach the light," then "perhaps the whimsical,
unpredictable, unexpected branches of Beauty will
make their way through and soar up to that very
place and...perform the work of all three." That's a
good image for women. Our branches were meant to
run wild. When we prune ourselves down,
straightening ourselves out, we look groomed, but
not beautiful.

We want to be true. Our flesh just needs
something more potent to assuage it. Try bringing a
lecture on good theology to a bitch, and she'll glare at

you. She knows she needs to wrangle with more than sound teaching to settle her down. The bitch may smile, but she quickly dismisses instruction on Christian Living, knowing that she's tried about as hard as she can to be good. She can't do it. And she's pretty sure she doesn't want to.

Our branches were meant to run wild, and when they do we will be beautiful. But also we will fail. Another way of saying this is: beauty is passionate and alive, so beautiful women, while life-giving and free, run the risk of hurting others, offending and failing. Truly beautiful women fail. We work so hard to cover over our impurity that our passion—our very beauty—gets neutralized down to something palatable but not compelling.

As Emerson said, "Your goodness must have some edge to it, else it is none."

What Is Beauty?

Try to define beauty. No, really—take a minute and try. It is simply not possible. I can try to tell you about the vibrant sunrise on the Colorado horizon this morning, but even if I spent seven paragraphs doing so, we both would know it is futile—you won't gasp the way I did when I opened our bedroom blinds. Try to describe the quirky smile on your toddler's face at breakfast, the kindness in the eyes of a woman you respect, or the alto line of the score of *La Traviata*. It can be enjoyable to *try*, but even if you find words with great precision and clarity, you know that you have failed. Beauty cannot be captured—it can only be responded to.

The closest we can come to when defining beauty is through synonyms. The word *glory* is a good synonym, but the poor word has been butchered and now carries all kinds of religious connotations. Glory is falsely thought of as something roused up in charismatic fervor, or shouted aloud, or worn on a face like magical face powder. As C.S. Lewis humorously says of this distortion—which he calls "luminosity"—"who wishes to become a kind of living electric light bulb?"[1]

No, we can all discern the difference between make-up and radiant skin. We can discern the difference between a roused-up, put-on glory and the true thing—when our faces shine and our eyes are bright because we've been deeply loved. Glory can also be falsely thought of as a competitive drive to be famous. Just thumb through *People* magazine and there it is in spades—the thirst for glory, the driving force in our culture. That is not beauty, of course. But that drive is a counterfeit, a knock-off of the original. We were designed to want to be noticed and seen. Again, Lewis speaks so well of this: "no one can enter heaven except as a child; and nothing is so obvious in a child—not in a conceited child, but in a good child—as [her] great and undisguised pleasure in being praised."[2] We were meant to be lauded and enjoyed. God did not put his image in us for it to be shrouded. He likes to notice us, and he loves when we enjoy being seen and delighted in.

The word *goodness* is also a fair synonym, but it is also a word which has lost its origins. Don't think of folded hands and correct manners; think of the things that stir your desire to become more like that which is good, things that make you want to live more fully, more in keeping with your true heart, and you'll find something that carries God's DNA, his beauty.

The original Hebrew word for glory, *kavod,* means the weighty presence of God as he is (nothing false about it). True glory is something that undoes us because of its purity, light, love and intimacy. Glory exposes; it reveals the truth about us—our loveliness and our shame. True glory unveils us, shows us off. And exposes.

Throughout this book, when we speak of beauty, we are speaking of a grand collision between the glory of God within you and the particularity of the beauty set within *your* heart. I don't carry your beauty, and you don't carry mine. We both manifest Jesus differently. The glory we are referring to is the life of God which shows up in your way in the world—your touch, your humor, your intellect, your physique, your style, your way with men, your way with women, your sensuality, your brand of kindness, what *you* look like when your heart burns against injustice.

Beauty is not something to be attained. It is to be released, un-tethered from the deepest place within us, set free from the echo chambers of the *safety* of Eden where our hearts were free to display the image of God—to embody the kavod of God, to be passionate, playful, intentional, creative, disruptive, substantial, unguarded, soft and caring, without any pressure to be those things.

Outside of Eden's safety, however, it is a different story. I have tried hard to be beautiful. I've tried to talk myself into the truth that I am beautiful. I have tried to rouse my heart, to cheerlead myself toward something good. May I say it again? It doesn't work. My beauty—the original glory placed in me like a fingerprint—has to be *restored*. As we will explore, there's much at war within you—many things that combat the glory of God. Our beauty has been ignored, mocked, violated, manipulated, and harmed. And in turn, we betray our own beauty—we attempt to erase, diminish and even abuse our own beauty. You can't change your heart through sheer will. We must allow the original image to be unveiled, allow the original glory to rise, again and again. Thankfully the image of God within you refuses to ever be completely erased, and thankfully the stunning grace of God when you are brutal with yourself and those you love never dies.

True beauty comes and finds us and laughs that we were looking the other way. We as women have brilliant strategies for looking the other way. Fear and Control. Pride and Contempt. Addiction and Deadness. These giants rise in our hearts perpetually, surfacing in sophisticated ways when we are able to hide them and in humiliating ways when we can't. And, as we will explore each one in the sections of this book, these strategies are often the natural result of our very hard stories.

Indestructible Women

Ranier Rilke, a German poet in the early 1900s, writes,

Ah, women, that you should be moving
Here, among us, grief-filled,
No more protected than we, and nevertheless
Able to bless like the blessed.
One who knows distances
Out to the outermost star
Is astonished when he discovers
Your magnificent heartspace.

Rilke humorously contrasts the essence of men and women. Even those most egalitarian among us can laugh along with him:

We, as if broken from chards
Even as boys, too sharp
at the edges, although perhaps
sometimes skillfully cut;
We like pieces of rock
that have fallen on flowers.

You, who are almost protection
where no one protects. The thought of you
is like a sleepy shade tree
for the restless creature of the solitary man.
(Antistophes)

Don't you love that he sees it—that inextinguishable, inexplicable female quality that our unsafe world and stories, our worst behavior can't destroy? Rilke saw it in the women around him a century ago, and we see it today. No matter how hard we may become, no matter how frantic we have allowed ourselves to be, no matter how dead we feel inside, or how despairing we are that we will ever feel okay within our own skin, we are meant to live out of our magnificent heart-space. We were meant to provide shade for others by our presence alone, and what we were created for will always show up, somehow, if even just a hint or glimmer of the intended thing.

The hint and glimmer can't be crushed. Even by pieces of rocks on our flowers. As the scripture says, "A broken reed I will not crush and a flickering wick I will not extinguish" (Matthew 12:20). In women, Beauty itself is always bigger than our foolish ways, our lack of goodness, our trying too hard.

Indestructible Beauty

Beauty always trumps bitch. But beauty also always trumps, *period*. Not just in a woman's heart, but in every way its indestructible quality shows up in our dark world.

There's a huge mining scar on the foothills above Colorado Springs. If you solely stare at it, or maybe with the surrounding hills which have been blackened by two furious wildfires, all you see is destruction. But if you back up and allow the entire range to come into view, you'll suddenly take in the gorgeous red rock formations of the Garden of the Gods, the sweeping, deep blankets of spruce and pine still fully intact, and your eye will move with a rugged upsweep to the top of Pikes Peak, unshakable as it swims beneath the Colorado blue. The glory is woven in with the shadow of the destruction, and somehow the destruction fades.

The mountains are simply capable of swallowing up the damage—they have taken a hit, but the beauty still overtakes and holds that which, in and of itself, is ugly. Francis Schaeffer calls this world "glorious ruins"— ruins, for sure, but the original glory just can't be erased.

In the two accounts of creation in Genesis, what God creates is captured by the Hebrew phrase *tov' Me'od.*, which means overflowing goodness, beauty which overwhelms, a place of shalom. Shalom means far more than merely a peaceful place. As Cornelius Plantinga says, "shalom is universal flourishing, wholeness, and delight—a rich state of affairs…the way it is supposed to be." We experience the slightest moments of this wholeness every time we melt into a hug, taste a perfect bite of filet mignon, feel the swell of pride when watching our child dance, laugh uproariously, or slowly stretch after a non-interrupted sleep. All of these moments say to us, "This is as it was meant to be." We see shalom in its full regalia, though, when broken relationships are restored, when an orphan is adopted into a loving family, when bombastic words melt into apologies, when lasting peace treaties are signed, and when sorrow over the earth's condition leads to greater responsibility and leadership in environmental stewardship.

God thinks up a stunning place for us to live in, and then establishes the most splendid way of living within that beautiful place. Some have called this design the five pillars of shalom—order (light from night), beauty (*tov Me'od*), rhythm (work and rest), relationship (between Adam, Eve, and God), and responsibility (freedom in living well). Plantinga calls it "the webbing together of God, humans, and all creation in justice, fulfillment and delight." And when God told Adam and Eve to be fruitful and multiply, and to subdue and rule the earth, he was, in essence, saying, "Go have fun. Make this overwhelmingly beautiful place even more beautiful."

Oh, but these ruins. We've turned the intended, kind order into a disheveled heap of traffic rage, alarm clocks and sleeping pills. We've turned rhythm into cacophony of workout routines driven by pressure mixed with grueling travel schedules. Relationship has been reduced to poking around on the internet or snippets of conversation, sound-bites of opinion. Shalom has been saturated with shame. And we didn't make it more beautiful. Take one look at the trash dump that has formed in the convergence of our oceans, domestic violence statistics, weeknight TV, or the strained face of a starving child. Our ruins show that we "bereave and assault what God has made, and what he desired for us to make more beautiful…. [S]in is blamable human vandalism of these great realities and therefore an affront to their architect and builder."[3]

And yet, somehow, the stunning nature of God is never fully destroyed by us.

Somehow, a woman—who had lost all ability for sexual pleasure with her husband because of adolescent shame from the abuse of a youth pastor—discovers the fun of sex. Somehow, another woman who had developed a reputation as a finger-wagging nag remembers how nice it is to wait for gifts to be brought to her voluntarily. A woman who used to highlight what *wasn't* written in a birthday card to her, underscoring all that was missing or lacking in her family's attempt to praise her, now relishes even the simplest act of gratitude in her children. It is almost as if in the abject refusal of beauty to be destroyed, God puts his love in bold print and italics. Bryant Myers says, "From the day our first parents walked out of the garden, estranged from God, each other, and the earth itself, God has been at work redeeming the fallen creation, its people and its social systems. God's goal is to restore us to our original identity, as children reflecting God's image, and to our original vocation as productive stewards living together in just and peaceful relationships."[4] This artist refuses that his artwork be completely erased. This father refuses that his children completely lose their luster. One day the intended image will be restored completely, but in the meantime, *tov Me'od* cannot be destroyed completely.

Beauty always wins.

The Safety of Beauty

Don't you find that you can be open, vulnerable, receiving of others' enjoyment of you, giving without guardedness, when your heart feels *safe*? Obviously, your world is not safe. Sometimes it seems that the only safe place left on earth is sitting on the couch, by a fire, watching *Little Women*. That is why beauty is so mind-blowing—its indestructible quality cradles the heart, even in the worst of times, when the ominous fog of anxiety and fear crowd around our minds.

The stunning terrain of the high mountain desert served as a comforting, safe friend for me when I was young; its beauty was a balm to a bewildered and confused young heart, allowing me to lean into something steady, always there. I could count on the comfort it provided, and I needed comfort.

* * * * *

I remember the first time my family began what was to become a solid tradition in our family. I was eleven years old, and it was early October, at midday when we first trekked to the little village of Chimayo, nestled in the foothills of the Sangre de Cristo Mountains north of Santa Fe. We were a limping and bleeding family (a story which will become more clear as the book goes on), but when we loaded up the car to head to Rancho de Chimayo for a special family dinner outing, all was well for a while. When we came to the crest of the meandering road, the fire of golden cottonwoods smoldered in the valley floor. Chimney smoke carried wafts of pungent pinion into the arroyos, weaving through juniper and sage. Chamisa added dots of yellow to the perimeter of the village. Maple splashed red, here and there. The sun was long over the creviced mesas, accentuating every eroded pocket in the hillsides, its finger stretching to the top of Truchas Peak. Even if I had never heard a word about the Spanish and Native American beliefs in the sacredness of this territory, I would have intuitively known that where we lived was holy. The land itself asked me to contend with God.

The beauty of the land comforted me, even when my lungs sputtered for breath. No amount of internal struggle, rage, fear, bitterness, confusion or conflict could remain intact in the presence of such beauty. I share C.S. Lewis' sentiments: "And if nature had never awakened certain longings in me, huge areas of what I can now mean by the `Love of God' would never, so far as I can see, have existed."[5]

We passed the old wooden sign carved outside the church, "El Sanctuario de Chimayo," and my mom relayed the mythic reputation it had for its healing holy water. We pulled the Ford into the gravel parking lot of the restaurant, surrounded by groupings of olive trees and cottonwoods, and saw the adobe building bearing wood shutters, red geraniums cascading against clay from window boxes. A sampling of all of New Mexico showed up here—Hispanic, White and Pueblo Indian. We blended and comingled and never gave it a thought.

It was apparent who had driven from my hometown, Los Alamos, though. There was a slightly stuffy, subtly stiff quality to us. Maybe it was the bolo ties our men tended to wear—they may have been silver and turquoise, but they were donned on men who had spent the day with laser technology or plutonium processing, not out harvesting a field or laboring until sweat beaded on bronze skin. Maybe it was the way our women fretted over their food choices, or wore large brimmed hats to protect them from the sun. Whatever it was, was unmistakable.

There were warm, quiet conversations and tables filled with laughter. We smelled the familiar charred smell of small, corner adobe fires. The earthen walls were covered with intricate rugs woven by the Ortega family for generations. Red chile ristras hung close by. The smell of a deep fryer filled with sopapillas produced an instant anticipation of green chili enchiladas or chili rellenos.

But even at age eleven—for many reasons you will come to understand—I was uneasy and agitated in the presence of my family. We sat down at a lovely patio table, but within five minutes the jabs, sarcasm and contempt began to show up—not blatantly, but they showed up. My father sat silently, and as we felt our unmet longing for him, a thick uncomfortable cloud descended on us. My mother anxiously fretted about how much the meal would cost. In turn, I began to mimic my mother's eating habits, sarcastically mocking the way she unsteadily brought the guacamole to her mouth. I rolled my eyes at my father. I went from sarcastic to sullen—clearly embarrassed of my family, for no reason other than it was *this* family. What was happening in me was beyond pre-adolescent frustrating behavior. It was a fledgling bitch finding a way to navigate very unmanageable emotions in a family that was disconnected and unstable.

But even this fledgling bitch melted in the presence of the glory of Chimayo. My disappointed heart and my pithy and dour demeanor could not be sustained under the inextinguishable beauty of this place—in part because this place helped my family become something more like what a family should be. The warmth of the servers, all from the Hernandez family, began to soften us. The acoustic guitar quietly reverberating on Spanish tile, the winding clematis on the rod-iron windows in the old wood doors, the intensity of the heat from the chiles—all of this gave us the ability to have a kind conversation rather than our practiced contempt. I came to cherish these treks to Chimayo, because here we morphed into a family, as we gathered round the food we loved. The beauty of Rancho de Chimayo was a culinary salve holding our fractured family together for one more day.

* * * * *

Moments like this remind me of the famous line of T.S. Eliot, as he quotes Julian of Norwich, "All is well and all will be well and all manner of things will be well."[6] At Rancho de Chimayo, all was well, and I *did not need* to be a bitch. I looked across at my mother, a woman tortured by the demons of her own body's war with manic-depression and the unspoken shame in her own story, and I saw more than a woman who lived in chaos. I saw sweetness. I saw the light in her eye which soothed all of us. I looked across at my father, a hard, stoic man of few words, a man for whom I ached for connection, and as contentment softened the features of his face, I felt peace. This *all is well* table intrinsically invited us away from our disappointments and reminded us again that there is always something bigger, greater, more real, than the smaller stories in which we live.

Beauty finds us. It simply shows up. It shows up in the terrain around us.

Beauty shows up in a family tradition, a spontaneous song on a quiet morning in bed, or when we laugh at the sight of a hummingbird's bomber-like descent only to come to rest on a spindle of a blossom. It appears as we feel the elbow of the Spirit in our ribs as we catch ourselves in our most practiced prideful arrogance. It tips its hand as we weep sweet tears when we remember an exquisite grace granted to us during a lonely time.

Beauty is different for everyone. It also lingers in the bottle-filled room when a woman allows herself to admit the alcohol is not big enough to hold her heart, or as a friend said recently, "I'm just out of stuff that works." It pushes its way through the pulse of techno-music and comes to rest in the thoughts of the girl who realizes that the guy's thrusting toward her on the dance floor was more about her body and fantasy than it was about a genuine curiosity about who she is. She drives home alone, aching but beautiful.

Leith's Lament

My friend Leith is beautiful even when she is furious. Actually, especially when she is furious. And as you'll see, she has much to rage over. I have known only a handful of people in my life who live genuinely free of the false religious masks we all put on, or at least try on. Our female masks are milquetoast even when our true face is angry or bewildered for legitimate reasons—we're so afraid to *appear* bitchy, after all—but somehow Leith hasn't put on a palatable face. She doesn't hide when she feels hard or confused, and I'm grateful to her for that.

Simon Tugwell says, "Like runaway slaves, we either flee our own reality or manufacture a false self which is mostly admirable, mildly repossessing, and superficially happy." If I had Leith's reality, I would want to flee, and I'm pretty sure I would pretend that I trusted God when I knew full well I did not. Leith's daughter, Hadley, was born with only a portion of her brain, so Leith and her husband, Aaron, live saturated lives, tending to the needs of their other two children while loving their girl who, even as a young teenager, needed them to change her diaper, to wheel her from room to room, house to house, hospital to school to home. Hadley had no true functioning, but for the mystery of her profound presence—her sometimes angelic, sometimes hilarious, sometimes agitated presence in the room.

Leith refused to shut down. I write this as we head into the Easter season, making plans to see a Passion Play, a reproduction of the passion (in Greek, literally *suffering*) of Jesus. Leith is passionate. She suffers openly. On the road to her Golgotha, she has consistently been curious about me, genuinely wanting to know how I am. But she never hides when her day is full of excrement or when she just isn't sure God is even there.

But you see, that is the point. Even smack dab in the middle of furious doubt, the beauty of a good heart's search for true life is apparent.

More from Tugwell: "We hide…behind some kind of appearance which we hope will be more pleasing. We hide behind pretty faces which we put on for the benefit of our public. And in time we may even come to forget that we are hiding, and think that our assumed pretty face is what we really look like."[7] That kind of "toning down for good appearances" does not have a grip on Leith, though I'm sure at moments she wishes she did not appear quite so hot or cold. I've seen her look embarrassed after an outburst about God's lack of satisfying answers. But as the sheepish conviction flits across her eyes, she displays the very thing Jesus delights in, the thing so rare among most of us as women: she is not lukewarm. Her life embodies Albert Camus' words: "In the depth of winter, I finally learned that within me there lay an invincible summer." She has tried desperately to find her grateful heart, even when she broke her hand as she pounded the floor in fury. And the access she gives me (and so many others) to her unpolished process is precisely why she is beautiful. Her process reminds me of Jacob's proclamation to the "angel of the Lord" toward the end of a night of wrestling, "I will not leave until you bless me!" Such honest engagement may cause us to walk away limping from our wrestling, but we will bear a new identity, one which reflects a beautiful, intimate, true engagement with the heart of God.[8]

Hadley died after several trips to death's door. Each time she surfaced back to life, there was a collective, conflicted sigh—so glad to have her, so weary of caring for her precious, broken body. Leith's life, as she walked alongside her Haddie, has helped me understand the words of Paul: "We have this treasure in earthen vessels that the all surpassing greatness of the power would be from God, and not ourselves...always carrying about in the body the dying of Jesus, that the life of Jesus would be manifest in our mortal bodies" (2 Cor. 4:7).

I was noticing the other day how luminous Leith's eyes are, how they are void of bitterness. She carries this powerful treasure because of her honest wrestling. As I see her eyes, I marvel to think of the many months when all Leith could pray was, "F**k you, amen." It is a beautiful prayer, really. Leith joined the ranks of true psalmists, those who worship with their conflicted hearts, turning their faces toward God *with* their guttural doubt, rather than turning away from him, as if they needed to get the doubt cleared up before looking him in the eye. David and the other psalmists did not express only praise as we have come to think of it—positive, upbeat and pure. No, 65-75% of the Bible's psalms are songs of lament—expressions of confusion, loss and a bewilderment as to what to do with God.

And thankfully, God himself desired for these psalms to be included by the priests as songs of worship. God calls it worship to turn our faces toward him with our uncertain and sometimes brutal assessment of him. He wants our hearts, not our cleaned up attitudes. He invites us into his *kavod* because he knows that our hearts will not want to stay bitter in the presence of his loving reception of our rage. Leith didn't want to stay in her fury, but she had to pass through it in order to be the woman she is.

It is terribly freeing to be loved by a woman who sometimes swears like a sailor and is a noble woman bearing the life of Christ.

Elena's Elegy

The bitch in all of us simply has one goal: protect the wounded self. Sometimes she is steely eyed, red faced and overtly mean. Sometimes she is sweeter than sweet, to the point of nausea. Either way, *the bitch flourishes in self-protection.* She is determined to stay safe on her own terms.

If you could glimpse the eyes of Elena, a power-house of a woman in Niger, you would see the tenacity of beauty on one of the most full and jovial faces you would ever find. Elena's large, rounded cheeks are dotted with freckles, so she looks like a cherub on a mission. She *is* on a mission: her heart blazes to bring young girls out of slavery.

But that blazing beauty has not always been there. Elena had to reclaim it. She will admit that this beauty is there in spite of her personal variety of bitch—one more subtly hard than overtly mean, more the nauseously sweet variety.

Elena was a graduate student in chemistry when a professor and mentor took special interest in her work. He asked her to be a part of a research project he was working on, and in the process he garnered her trust and prompted her to begin telling him intimate details of her life and heart. Over time he began to sexually exploit her, threatening her education and grades should she refuse. The betrayal and confusion made a strong home in Elena's heart, and she resigned herself—no, she *committed* herself—to a quiet and passive existence, with a deep vow to never be tricked or wounded again. She became a very hard woman, but her hardness was experienced more as feigned kindness than raging mania.

Elena is a great example of a sweet bitch, a woman who seems kind until you try to get to know her. It is then the daggers come, usually in resistance, deflection of affection and curiosity, an overall message of *stay away*. Her resolve to not hope for much, live too loud, to not attract attention in order to stay safe turned her passionate, fiery, jovial self into a lifeless, limp dismissible, cold bitch. Her sullen face looked perpetually disappointed and sour.

Elena could not have known how the fire of beauty within her would be rekindled when she began to learn about the exploitation of young girls, especially those trafficked out of West Africa. Her heart broke for them, and out of its shattered pieces flowed a passion that would not allow her heart to remain sullen. Problem was, in order to follow her passion, she had to face her own story. Her heart had to break for *herself.* She could not remain a bitch and at the same time trek into the courageous endeavor of loving. She had to betray her strategy, break her vow with self-protection, betray her bitch, come out of hiding, and do something. She got a graduate degree in theology, not so she could talk more clearly about God, but so she could embody him more beautifully as she gives her life to creating alternative incomes and job skills and counseling and restoration to girls forced into prostitution.

Deadness didn't win for Elena. Her beauty did. Her war with sullen, sticky sweet falseness is sometimes there, but it just doesn't have the power to overshadow a lively, jovial woman who, though terrified, risks daily.

Sarai's Story

I was in Starbucks recently and glanced at a *New York Times* headline about exploitive working practices in the Caribbean. Later that day I glimpsed Pulitzer Prize-winning Nicholas Kristof on *Oprah*, and was struck by his personal courage in not only writing about but also involving himself personally and financially in the rescue of some enslaved girls in Cambodia. While making dinner I caught a CNN report by Anderson Cooper about a woman from the Ukraine trafficked to Dubai for sex with international businessmen. I am, like many, deeply moved by these stories. We hear a trafficker shamelessly say, "If I sell an ounce of cocaine I profit only once, but if I sell a woman, I can do it numberless time," and of course we are horrified. The financial rationale is impeccable. The evil behind the remark is chilling. We know that what we have just heard and witnessed has the weight to undo us if we let it.

But these stories have become common in our consciousness. I am hesitant to write about the bitch inside a Thai friend named Sarai because her story has become a familiar one, almost to the point of desensitization. But hers is not just another story. Sarai understands why her story should undo us.

Sarai has a slight frame, but her rage caused her to look leviathan-like as she pushed one of her counselors to the ground, screaming, "You don't know a f**king thing about my life! Leave me alone!" It wasn't just outbursts that showed her hardness, though. She lived many years with an intractable scowl on her face, one that would only intensify if you approached her with kindness. Her heart was like a steel-trap door. Yet, if you sat with her today, you'd be with a kind, funny young woman.

Sarai knows the horror of the little beds in the red light district of Bangkok, because she spent much of her young life there. Sarai had several customers a night forced upon her, raping her from the time she was eleven. *Eleven.* Eventually, Sarai was rescued from her slave owner and brought to a home where she was offered restorative love.

We would think that she would be nothing but grateful, exhaling deeply into the warm bed of safety and care, right? Sarai was grateful for the rescue, but the act of responding to the care was too risky, too much to hope for. She was literally too tender to the touch. Sarai's heart and body had become so shut down that she raged against anyone who offered care, even the very care that would awaken her deadened heart. She, like all of us when we've been wounded, had to ease into risking again—risking that her heart was worth it, that love was actually intended for her, for her good. Slowly—years and years on—she realized that she was safe, that she could let down. She learned to receive, and to be the kind and funny person she always was. It started with needing to change her, sleep-in-the day habits, with allowing a simple conversation with a caretaker, with finally letting an older man to give her a clean, affectionate side hug.

Sarai's heart is still being softened. In many ways, she is finally being given a chance to grow up, to blossom in the presence of safety. She is flourishing and maturing. She says she wants to help other girls who have suffered as she has.

That's the inextinguishable beauty of God.

Beauty is always present, and it shows up most *along the way* as we yearn for it to win over the hardness of our heart. Sometimes it is hard won, but it always has the power to win.

Your story may not be as severe as Sarai's, but if beauty can win in her life, in Leith's life, and in my life, it can win in yours. My hope is that this book will make clear that we all have stories. We all have hardened. But we all can all be beautiful.

Beauty really can trump bitch.

---

[1] C.S. Lewis, *The Weight of Glory and Other Addresses* (New York: Touchstone, 1975), 32, 33.

[2] Lewis, *Weight of Glory*, 33.

[3] Cornelius Plantinga, *Not the Way It's Supposed to Be: A Breviary of Sin* (Grand Rapids: Eerdmans, 1995), 16.

[4] Bryant L. Myers, *Walking with the Poor: Principles and Practices of Transformational Development* (Maryknoll, NY: Orbis Books, 1999), 42.

[5] C.S. Lewis, *The Four Loves* (Orlando, FL: Harcourt Brace and Company, 1960), 20.

[6] T.S. Eliot, `Little Gidding' from "Four Quartets" in *Collected Poems, 1909-1962* (London: Faber, 1974).

[7] Simon Tugwell, *The Beatitudes: Soundings in Christian Tradition* (Springfield, IL,: Templegate Publishers, 1980), 130.

[8] Genesis 32 states that Jacob and "a man came and wrestled with him until the dawn began to break. When the man saw that he would not win the match, he touched Jacob's hip and wrenched it out of its

socket. Then the man said, "Let me go, for the dawn is breaking!" But Jacob said, "I will not let you go unless you bless me." "What is your name?" the man asked. He replied, "Jacob." "Your name will no longer be Jacob," the man told him. "From now on you will be called Israel, because you have fought with God and with men and have won." "Please tell me your name," Jacob said. "Why do you want to know my name?" the man replied. Then he blessed Jacob there. Jacob named the place Peniel (which means "face of God"), for he said, "I have seen God face to face, yet my life has been spared" (24-30).

Chapter Two

Control: Understanding Fear and Foundations

Woman was God's second mistake.

> ~ Friedrich Nietzsche

*Every woman should have four pets in her life.
A mink in her closet, a jaguar in her garage, a
tiger in her bed, and a jackass who pays for
everything.*

> ~ Paris Hilton

*If a woman shows too often the Medusa's head,
she must not be astonished if her lover is turned
into stone.*

> ~ Henry Wadsworth Longfellow

Fear not.

> ~ Jesus

Fear Gives Birth to Control

If beauty is so indestructible, why does it seem to disappear so quickly? If beauty can't be erased, why does my face change from soft to grimaced, my manner from respectful to commandeering, my best intentions to live a lovely life so quickly dissolve into old familiar tendencies of control? As I'll show you, my controlling nature wins so often that it is hard to believe that I am not simply controlling *at core*. The need to micromanage the world is woven into every other nuanced struggle I have to stay dignified, solid, attractive.

Based on my friendships and conversations I have with women in the counseling office (and their partners), I know I am not alone on this one. My beauty disappears into control, just as yours does, when I am living out of fear. Perhaps this is why the most-used phrase by Jesus is, "Fear not."

We all have scenes in our stories that instructed us that fear and control are the only smart responses. Our task is to trace those scenes for understanding about our fear so that it no longer rules us. It is good to name, to put words to our stories. Facing the particularities of your life simply helps you understand the particularity of the healing you need. If we consider the fearful scenes that become the birthplaces of our controlling ways, then we can dream more specifically of ways we can join the Life of God in rewriting the story, creating beauty where there was none. My hope is that as you trek with me into some particular scenes of my story for this purpose, you can begin to pinpoint moments in your own life that may be fueling the bitch inside of you. There's great hope in this: if healing is available (and it is), then beauty can be given more space to flourish.

My husband is a humble man with a deep heart. As I type this, Steve is outside tending to our spring garden, which is ablaze because he had the vision and foresight to put a slew of bulbs in the ground late last autumn. He went to town with those bulbs. I thought he was overdoing it a bit, that maybe the bulbs would take over our garden. But as I look out over the blanket of fuchsia, deep peach, magenta and yellow, I am quieted by the beauty residing in my husband's heart, and how the world is different because of his touch.

Steve is also a strong man, a presence. His career has taken him into the bowels of industry, where he navigates not only corporate leaders and their quirky pride, but also governments that are powerful, dark and oppressive. He has had to interact with polished, hardened faces of organized crime, making rough business decisions, contrary to profit, for the sake of protecting the exploited and the exploitable. His calling includes seeing, naming and navigating the ways of evil—unraveling the fabric in which it is woven into a person, a culture, a way of thinking. He has a keen eye for deception and little tolerance for falsehood. His North Star is goodness.

When goodness is threatened, or when a situation or conversation or interaction is playing out in a way which he discerns is not good, he can become intense. His voice is loud. He can look and sound intimidating. He is keenly aware of how he has used this intimidation throughout his life, and he grieves accordingly. Even so, he is a force to be reckoned with. And he is smart with his influencing words.

Sometimes in the presence of this intensity, I become a little girl. *Disintegrate* is a better word. I am reactive, defensive, and whiny. As you have heard, this little girl has been a horrifying embarrassment to me. She throws tantrums; she throws mugs. I knew she was there, but I had no idea how her trembling fear continued to fuel and inform my own furious need for control.

When I disintegrate into this little girl, it is because I am no longer seeing Steve's face. The love in his eyes (which is consistent and unchanging even when he is most frustrated) is lost to me in those moments. My eyes become blind to his love. When I disintegrate—when I, in the words of the Apostle Paul, "think and reason like a child"—I lose track of who it is I am with.

But if I take a moment to simply listen more carefully to what the young Jan is trying to say, I find she has a story to tell. She is eight years old. She is with her dad.

* * * * *

My father grew up in the Kansas heat in a home filled with Germanic stoicism and my grandfather's cold heart. Dad discovered my mom, a tender and diminutive brunette, in a high school lobby in 1938. They had been married sixty-five years when my mom passed away, and their life together was rife with drama and intensity—due mostly to my mom's dark and agitated days from manic-depression. Dad studied at MIT through the Army Corp of Engineers and was a twenty-two year-old father when he received special orders to trek with two other young scientists to a location in the West for purposes undisclosed until they arrived.

He arrived in the makeshift mountain community of Los Alamos and discovered that he was to design the detonation system for the Manhattan Project (the atomic bombs eventually dropped on Hiroshima and

Nagasaki). You can imagine the pressure. Working in a community that included men such as Robert Oppenheimer, Enrico Fermi and occasional consultation with Albert Einstein proved to be exhilarating, but the nature of the project and the sobriety of the war effort took its toll.

I do not know what it was that fueled my dad's detachment or prompted his rage. After the war ended, he and Mary raised six children over a span of twenty years. I was number six, birthed when Mary was forty-five years old. Was it the pressure of his highly classified work? Was it his own father's harm of his heart? Or maybe the baseline for folks in his generation that offered little space for more difficult emotions? Surely there was the consistent stress of riding out my mother's unstable moods and having to kick into emergency mode when she needed psychiatric hospitalization, often for lengthy periods of time.

I don't know which of these caused my father to explode, as his story goes unnamed by him to this day. But I do know there was a refusal in him to own his actions, and this was deeper than the generation he was a part of, deeper than his personality, deeper than his tough lot with mom. He simply refused to look at his life or his impact on his children. He camped with us. He loved to garden and shared that passion with me. His tenacious commitment to mom was noble and underappreciated. He was a man of beauty in many ways. He was also a cauldron of unpredictable fury.

When I was eight, I was backed up against a thin kitchen cabinet. The cabinet moved a bit as my back slid down and I came to rest on the floor, making me aware of its flimsy construction. I pulled my knees against my face, my hands held out to shield myself from my father's hot contempt. I had asked for his attention, and when the request was met with lengthy silence, I began whining for his attention. I had forgotten, in my desire for him to see some ladybugs I had placed in a jar, that my dad was accessible only when he decided that he was accessible. I forgot for too long, persisted too much, and he became enraged to the point of standing over me with fire in his eyes. Heat emanated from him, and as his feet moved, he caused me to cower. My neck was wet and I was heaving—deep breaths, sobs. I don't know when I started crying, but I did know he was screaming: "Quit crying! Quit your crying! I don't want to hear about it! Quit whining! Quit crying!"

I gathered my tears for this round of humiliation. I mustered the courage to look up, only to find dad standing there, silent, a look of deep disgust in his eyes. I was such a disappointment to him. He left the room, saying nothing, taking with him his fearful presence and his contempt.

* * * * *

Clearly this scene is one of the birthplaces of significant fear. And fear has birthed a septic space within my heart.

Cynthia Monahan has a definition of trauma: *the occurrence of the unthinkable*. I have often said that anything outside of perfect love, anything outside of Eden, is unthinkable. Eden is the baseline. So anything that provokes fear is definitively unthinkable. That I would have to cower before my father is unthinkable, as it is for any child who has fear in the presence of a parent. In Eden it was not so.

Triggered Control

In love we are swept off our feet; in trauma our legs are knocked out from under us. ~ Peter Levine

Yesterday I had an interaction with a client that got me all worked up inside. Near the end of our counseling session, he looked skeptically at me in response to something I said. There was a slight mockery on his face as he subtly rolled his eyes at me. Now, this kind of dismissive attitude is not good and likely needs to be addressed in his life, but internally my reaction was completely out of proportion to his momentary dismissal of me. If you crawled up inside my head at that moment, you would have found a whirling dervish of confusion. I became cloudy, uncertain, and unsteady. This insecurity—which felt so *familiar*—caused me to become very defensive inside. I was scrambling to find my footing.

By the time my client and his wife left my office, I was in the disintegration process I told you about. There was something about the experience of being dismissed that caused what felt like an avalanche inside of me, taking me back to a younger, more threatening time.

Have you ever had the experience of feeling or behaving in a way in which, moments later, you found yourself asking, "What just happened?" I am guessing you have. We have all had moments when our thoughts or behavior feel involuntary, when our reactions are *way* beyond what is reasonable for the situation at hand. We might see our irrational reactivity in hindsight, but in the moment we don't see it at all. Though these moments often feel hazy, if we pay close attention to them, we become aware that we were taken back to an experience that has little to do with the current moment.

After the session with my client, I took some time to think about what had prompted the charged response in me, and I realized that when I was young, my father often dismissed me, and the look and tone in my client was reminiscent of my father's mockery. Sometimes we hear a certain word, spoken in a certain inflection, see a certain look on a face or experience a certain smell or sound, and we are taken back almost completely to moments of trauma. Trauma occurs when we experience a fight-or-flight response in the presence of abandonment or danger. If, in the present, we experience something that prompts memory—literal brain pathways—of that abandonment or danger, something deep within us tells us to fight like crazy or hide in the rocks. It is a very disorienting and frightening experience. And when we are disoriented and frightened, we usually get defensive and self-protective.

Psychologists call this involuntary process "triggering." In a very real way, there is nothing to be done about it, meaning we cannot control when we are triggered back into a place of trauma. But there is a lot we can do in response to the trigger itself. If you have had this experience—and we all have—don't despair. There is a lot of good that can come from recognizing your trauma triggers.

I get triggered in my marriage when I sense even a hint of intensity in Steve. I flood with fear, and I see the wrong face—I see my father. My father and Steve are deeply and fundamentally different men. Steve can be intense, but his heart is kind and malleable. My father is not merely an intense man; he is destructive in his red-hot rage. When we are triggered, we don't see anything accurately. It is terribly unfair to be seen through wounded eyes, to find your own face being viewed as the face of someone harmful. I have failed Steve many times (unwittingly, as we will see) when in my triggered state I am back in the past, in the presence of my raging father, and am reactive with Steve as a result. Steve becomes the falsely accused villain, the target of my reactivity. In those moments, I forget that I am with a man with a heart of gold who does not deserve to be related with in a defensive manner.

What are your triggered moments? Is it when you see disappointment in someone's eyes and experience it as though you completely and utterly failed? Is it when you sense irritation in someone and are convinced you are nothing but a big irritant in the world? Do you pick up on anger and immediately feel like you want to run out of the room? It is as if a kitten walks in the room and we see the jowls of a tiger.

I don't know what your triggers are, but I know you have them, because none of us live in this world without experiencing some level of trauma. If you let them, those moments can bring you face to face with how you want to engage your story, seeking Jesus' healing touch on your neglected and undressed wound. But when we leave our triggered moments un-dealt with—that is, if we attempt to ignore them or believe that nothing can be done about them—we disrespect our capacity for beauty. If we learn to catch ourselves when we are operating out of triggered fear, then we can recognize the injustice we have brought to our husband, friend, mother, sister. If we (attempt to) ignore our triggered moments, we begin to live from what we will call "triggered control," a term that refers to the habit of reacting relationally out of unhealed places inside of us, *allowing the triggered response to reign, rule and have a life of its own.*

We must, quite simply, confess the harm we do, even when we are triggered. Then we can search for a deeper healing for those reactive places.

The Fear We Carry in Our Bodies

There is a mountain of brain research and clinical evidence to indicate that your trauma is a far more pervasive component in your behavior than you might think. The purpose of this discussion is not to give a comprehensive lesson on trauma responses, but to help you see that your struggle is often involuntary and understandable from a physiological standpoint (in the traumatic triggering), and to also to invite you to research for yourself, to seek out an understanding of your behavior so that you can address it and seek the healing you need, body and soul.

Think back to Sarai, the young woman in Thailand. For her to trust the pleasure of being cared for in a loving, life-giving way, she had to learn to trust her physiology. Another way to say it is: she had to push past the alarm bells that ring "danger, danger, danger" when her body feels responsive to life. Trauma causes all our systems to fire. Our autonomic and sympathetic nervous system, our adrenal system, and our hormonal system are put on high alert when we are traumatized. Later in life, when we are safe and away from trauma, when we are aroused by anything—touch, love, anger—our systems can get triggered into a state of danger again, even when there is nothing to fear. Sarai's healing began as she slowly, little by little, chose to not circumvent the enjoyment, nor sabotage the pleasure of love.

Peter Levine states:

> Traumatized people have a deep distrust of the arousal cycle, usually for good reason. This is because to a

trauma victim, arousal has become (physiologically—brain chemically) coupled with the overwhelming experience of being immobilized by fear. Because of this fear, the traumatized person will prevent or avoid completion of the arousal cycle, and remain in a cycle of fear.

Think of this cycle of fear simply as your determination to not be too stirred by anything or anyone in any direction emotionally, spiritually, physically. Levine goes on to say, "When we can trust the arousal cycle and are able to flow with it, the healing of trauma will begin."[9] I don't know what risk you might want to take to trump this fear, but something as small as not bracing when someone attempts to hug you, or saying "thank you" when someone notices how lovely you look, is a good place to start.

Chronic Control

I love my marriage. I'm a marriage counselor who works toward inner transformation rather than from tips and techniques. I am fairly respected in our community. I work with women's hearts, married and single, all the time. I live in a community that values living authentically, from a whole heart. For over thirty years, I've been given the most exceptional resources Christendom can offer. I've been mentored by the best, believed in and known by really great leaders, and I am grateful for a trustworthy, true reputation.

Blah, blah, blah.

As I have said, some days I feel like I am the most beautiful woman in the world. Steve relishes the gifts he receives on those days. But the truth is that on bad days I am also the woman who harps on him over many things he does and the choices he makes about how he will spend his day. Nagging is too innocuous of a word to describe what I do. I speak to him as if he were a child. I never thought I would be "that" woman, but I am that woman on steroids.

I am tempted, as I tell you this, to laugh about it, to make light of it. But I can't. I am just beginning to see the impact my controlling nature, my controlling *choices,* have on Steve's heart. If he was not the man he is, loving and strong enough to stand in my way when I'm like that, he would end up feeling demeaned, emasculated and condescended to. He should. I treat him as if he needs me to think for him—not exactly what causes a man (or anyone for that matter) to come alive.

I lived a lifetime before marrying. Steve and I married when I was forty-four. I have spent ample time (perhaps more than anyone should) naming my story and cultivating self-understanding, so I naively believed that a previous struggle with control would not rule me when we said our vows.

So what happened? Why is that, for the first year of our marriage, the bitchy, controlling, frightened girl surfaced as if from the deep caverns of the mines of Moria? You might recall the moment in *The Lord of the Rings* when the hobbits accidentally drop something into a deep underground cavern in the formerly dwarf-inhabited mines of Moria, waking the evil orks which were sleeping there. Yeah, it was like that. All new marriages are fraught with adjustments, of course—relinquishing independence, learning to share a bathroom—but this was different. Something dark had been dormant in me, and wow, did marriage wake it up.

To know what exactly was dormant, we must revisit young Jan when she was fourteen.

This time we find me fleeing the presence of my detached, raging father, and my sweet but agitated, paranoid mother who leaned into me for companionship and comfort…

* * * * *

I ran out the front door under a sky aglow with the last hint of evening crimson. The Sangre de Cristo Mountains were washed in the purple hue that gave them their name. The thunderheads that had rolled over the Pajarito plateau that afternoon now hung over Taos—big, charcoal marshmallows. It was the kind of beauty that turns up the level of joy, and also the level of pain, if you let it. My chest ached. I needed to move. I stretched my legs against the curb in a runner's stretch and ran until the moon's light began to hang over the dark stretches of road above the Rio Grande. I stopped, sweat building on my forehead. I had been running a long time. Winded, I sat down on a rock beside the road and looked up at the growing blanket of stars. My endorphins held back the empty pit that attempted to surface. Everything was okay for a moment. Everything would die down. We'd be okay. My ritual had again saved me once again.

* * * * *

I made it better. I found a way to regain some composure by fleeing the home that caused me to often disintegrate. I discovered that beauty would bring me some peace for a while. The dilemma was: this simple experience of running at fourteen became but one of thousands of times that I fled my circumstance through some form of rigor. And there was always more to be had. The beautiful rhythms of exercise became brutal rigors of relentless workouts on no more than 300 calories a day, a classic obsession with weight and diet, a humiliated cycle of starvation, binging, and more starvation.

By the time I was 22, an eating disorder had provided me with a strong, fortressed self-protection, and it also had built arrogance in me. You tend to get arrogant when you figure out a way to outrun your insecurity. I convinced myself I had created a world where there was no risk for my heart whatsoever. Illusion, yes, but I was determined.

As I prepared to marry Steve, I reflected back with gratitude for the healing I had found in my twenties and thirties from the heavy, debilitating, and septic need for constant control. The addiction had given way to an acknowledgement of feelings, longings and sorrow. I had grieved, received counseling, and felt a genuine touch from God as I fought hard to extricate myself from the clutches of the disorder. It took years, but I walked out of those years with dignity and a deep compassion for other women trapped in this self-absorbed, painful prison. By the time I married Steve, the struggle with control was almost non-existent. I had for a long time lived free from the ruminating obsessions, fear-based thinking, insecurity, and need to prove myself. It honestly wasn't a primary part of the template of my life any longer.

And then…Steve and I got married. And those places inside of me so desperately in need of care when I was fourteen rose up like tender jonquils reaching for the warmth of Steve's love. Though my neglected heart had been tended to through the years by a rich community of friends, the kind touch of God through music, the love of dogs, gardening, and prayer, at core that young part of me lay dormant in a place inside called Reserved for the One with Whom You Are Safe. My father was not safe, so I found a way to become the safest place on earth within myself.

Now, with Steve, my heart was once again in the hands of someone who could either care for me or fail me, simply because I had chosen to place my heart in his care. Would he see me, really? Could I trust him, really? Would he care about my needs, thoughts, opinions...really? Would he put down his newspaper to listen to me, or should I just start whining right away, beat him to the chance to let me down? Should I exhale and relax into the risky business of waiting for him to be curious about me, or should I garner my skills, my self-sufficient, fear-drenched skills, and pick and prod and tear down, so that there was no risk whatsoever?

Chronic control means living in the patterns we create to make our life work. They are commitments hewn into the brain pathways of our thinking, and they are tended to like a temple shrine in South Asia. We visit the control so often, throwing it trinkets and performing our rituals around it, that it becomes a way of being. My rigor, the descent I made into the manipulatively controlled relationship with exercise, food, or obsession with my body fat became the most controllable god I could create. This god brought comfort without having to face my heart's questions, or my heart's false conclusion that God had abandoned me to the chaos, that it was up to me to get ahold of the situation.

The Spirit of Fear

The Spirit of Fear paralyzes in a frustrating, vague, unnamed fog. If you are in relationship with someone who lives from a Spirit of Fear, you live with a cocktail of weakness, hatred and an instability that makes it difficult to rest or to enjoy your loved one peacefully. Agitation is often in the air. And you can't quite pinpoint whether the source of the agitation is them or you.

If fear and its accompanying need for control are birthed in the presence of rage, then a Spirit of Fear is born out of the more subtle context of abandonment and neglect. A Spirit of Fear is cultivated over time, in the overarching theme of the script, the lighting, the soundtrack, the backdrop. The air the character breathes is neglect, and by mid-story the Spirit of Fear captivates the audience with its pungency.

I grew up breathing that air. It is a confusing wound, hard to pinpoint or nail down, and that is what produces the deep conflict of fear—trusting and not trusting, not knowing what to trust.

Consider little Jan again. As you read through this scene when I was four years old, listen for the not-so-obvious backdrop of neglect. What do you hear that I needed? How do you see my heart reasoning with how alone I was? Are there similar scenes or seasons in your own life?

* * * * *

The dust was already hot in the morning sun. I had just learned to skip—a trot, really, which came in handy so my bare feet would not burn on the canyon floor. I didn't have my shoes; guess I forgot them. The trail was well worn, but occasionally a small rock or a dry pine needle was enough interruption to cause me to stop and dust off the bottom of the four-year-old feet which had, by any adult's estimation, already traveled way too far from home.

I was looking for my brothers – I had heard them talking this morning about coming down here, but so far all I saw was dry ponderosa and chalky cliffs, spotty sunshine. It felt like a scene from one of my storybooks. A squirrel chattered at me and I craned my neck to see where it was. His reprimand was coming from a high branch in a ponderosa pine— mocking, laughing at me. When spoken to in a quiet voice, the intense squawking ceased.

I plopped down on a fresh bed of pine needles and contemplated the ground, the ants, the sap that formed like a plug over a wounded branch. I pulled myself close and stuck my finger in, surprised by its texture. The smell reached me before I could pull my fingers to my nose. An "ahhhh" let loose from me, a startle. Attempts to wipe the sap off onto my gingham shorts produced only little balls on my hands, now collecting dirt. Sleepiness came almost instantly. With heavy eyes, I found a decent sunspot against the trunk of an old log, which resembled a crinkled old man. Repositioning my head to avoid a calloused lump in the trunk, I snuggled close to where his chest and arms were and drifted, dreamless.

The squirrel spoke again. Its chatter drew me from the void of heavy, dark sleep and into the smells of the canyon. I rolled over in the shadow falling in the canyon, and a horrible feeling descended on me. Was it lunchtime? Snack time? Naptime? Dread is an awfully grown-up emotion; I did not even know what it was.

Disoriented and stiff, I caught a glimpse of where I had come from. Panic filled me as I saw that the shadow had grown long, so I burst into a full gallop back toward the canyon wall, ignoring every prick under my feet. Breathless, I looked up. The trail to our home was a serpentine line, straight up the canyon wall. I did not remember descending such a thing. Coming down I had only one thing on my mind—explore and find my brothers. I had moved so fast, the slippery, worn volcanic rock didn't faze me. A pounding began in my chest. Frantically but carefully, as a scared deer might before making a leap across a large river, I paused with determination.

Grabbing hold of a scraggly bush, firmly rooted between cracks in the black rock, I lifted myself onto the trail. My bare feet felt the ground, which had lost its heat since the sun left the canyon. Step by step, shrub by shrub, straining my forming quadriceps, my foot slipping occasionally, producing a small avalanche of dust and pebbles, I stopped to rest on a level patch. Looking up, it was clear that my goal was within sight, but between me and the house was a sheer wall of dirt, above which could only be seen a cobalt blue sky, the color of early evening. I could envision the scene on the other side of the horizon above my head—a patch of freshly mowed summer lawn, a slab of concrete covered with colored hopscotch drawings, and my swing set. I plunged one foot into the dirt wall, pushed and reached up, grabbed the top edge with both hands, and pulled my little body up over the edge, resting my ribs over the rim. Then came my last ascent: pushing my hands underneath me, pulling myself onto level ground. Suddenly my face was surrounded by the soft caress of grass. I rolled over, looking directly up, away from the whole ordeal. I did not say a word. Rolling again onto my stomach, I arched my back and looked around, expecting a rush of love to come my way: "Where have you been? We've been looking all over for you! We were so worried! We are so glad you are okay!" What I found was silence but for the buzz of a latent summer fly.

I got up, dusted off the front of my shorts, and wandered inside. The scene itself was serene: Dad watching TV, my brothers building a ship in a bottle, my sister reading. The stillness, the lack of commotion, the sheer *all seems well* of the moment dizzied me. I felt the conception of a boulder in my belly, one which would, throughout my life, grow to the full measure of my gut. It was rock hard, laced with the dynamite of confusion, the bewilderment of a child's need colliding with a presumed independent maturity. Mom was peeling boiled potatoes for potato salad in the kitchen. She looked up, briefly, from her task. She noticed me and went back to her dazed, methodic peeling. She said nothing.

"Mommy, what time is it?"

" . . . "

"Mommy?"

"Uh…oh. It is about seven o'clock. Dinnertime."

* * * * *

49

This example is perhaps easy to hear. There is a temptation to simply think of me as the fiercely independent child, but anyone with a heart can see that I was a *child*, simply a girl who needed supervision, attention, care. Neglect, where the soil of a Spirit of Fear is cultivated, does not only happen in tenement housing or low-income barrios (though of course it can be there as well). Suburbia is often rife with neglect cloaked in the pressure-filled, saturated, driven lives of parents. Sometimes it's the result of addiction or mental illness. The point is, it is not *uncommon*. Neglect is the most common form of child maltreatment.[10] Sometimes it is obvious, and sometimes it is found in a context like the one I just described. Neglect makes room for fear to visit a little heart, interpreting the world for them, saying, "If you allow your heart to rise, you will find *nothing* there to meet it. If you trust this person to care for you, to stay, you are a fool among fools. You thought perhaps there was love for you. You have tasted a bit of love and have been duped that it is truly real. Do something, quick, for you will taste in this moment the bitter acid of abandonment. *You are about to be failed.*"

One of the best illustrations of how fear comes to interpret our experience for us as children is the experience of Hushpuppy, the little girl in the movie *Beasts of the Southern Wild,* who lives in a severely neglectful environment in the community below the levees around New Orleans. Her mother is gone, her father is dying of AIDS, and she is drastically vulnerable in a world saturated with alcohol and no supervision. She feigns independence. We laud her resilience, but our heart breaks for her fear. No movie that I have seen captures more clearly how a child reasons with the unreasonable. When a child is afraid (and she was, all the time, with no one was giving her words for it), and her world is out of control, she tends to blame herself. Hushpuppy's self-blame took the form believing that whole glaciers would crash down, destroying the world if she made a wrong move. Where did Hushpuppy come up with *that*?

Evil is not always obvious, but it is predictable. Evil always brings an interpretation to us—a way of making sense of the world when no one is helping us make sense of it. The strategy is amazing, and it generally works.

The way evil predictably comes to us to falsely reinterpret our story is illustrated well in the character of Ms. O'Brien in the series *Downton Abbey*. I'm amazed at how well this maid to Lady Grantham embodies the way evil quietly comes up and plays on our fear and offers a false interpretation ("Hmmm…do you really think you'll be okay if you don't take matters into your own hands?"), and then slips away to do her chores, having planted seeds of destruction.

Evil wants us to defend our frightened hearts in our own power. If I listen to the false interpretation, of course I am going to clamp down in defense of my soon-to-be-failed heart.

The Power of Love

When Hushpuppy was afraid, which was often, she had visions of prehistoric Aurox tracking her. This is such a great picture to me of how our fear haunts us, follows us, wanting us to believe our false reasoning about the world. Hushpuppy had to stare down her Aurox fears, but she did not know how. There's a beautiful scene in the movie when Hushpuppy encounters a woman who picks her up and holds her for a lingering moment. Hushpuppy relishes the moment, drinks it in like water. She is parched for what she calls "being lifted," and this woman is lifting her. It is one of the only tangible pictures of love that Hushpuppy has, and the power of that one encounter in her life is astounding. Hushpuppy charges out of that scene with a newfound ability to stare down the Aurox. As the monsters of fear predictably track her, this time Hushpuppy, with her little hands on her hips, stares one of them down, and it slowly kneels down in front of her, tamed.

Love is a powerful antidote to fear.

Steve's love has been a tremendous drink of water for me. But the love of a partner, friend, or mentor is not big enough to supply the kind of love for which our wounded hearts ache. The Apostle John writes some of my favorite words:

> We know how much God loves us, and
> we have put our trust in his love. God is
> love, and all who live in love live in
> God, and God lives in them. And as we

live in God, our love grows more perfect. So we will not be afraid on the Day of Judgment, but we can face him with confidence because we live like Jesus here in this world. Such love has no fear, because perfect love expels all fear. If we are afraid, it is for fear of punishment, and this shows that we have not fully experienced his perfect love. We love each other because he loved us first" (I John 3:15-18).

John is Jesus' friend, and John gets it. He knows we have not experienced the kind of love, nurture, attachment, that allows us to feel safe. Earlier in this letter he says this:

For the darkness is disappearing, and the true light is already shining. If anyone claims, "I am living in the light," but hates a brother or sister, that person is still living in darkness. Anyone who loves another brother or sister is living in the light and does not cause others to stumble. But anyone who hates another brother or sister is still living and walking in darkness. Such a person does not know the way to go, having been blinded by the darkness.

There was a day when I would have read those words and felt only discouraged at how little I love.

But John is trying to encourage us, to cheer us on, to tell us, "I know you want to be loving. Hang on, the light is coming to those dark and bound-up terrified places. You don't know where to go, but I'll come and find you." Deep inside of me there's been a little girl hiding in, caught in, blinded by darkness. She doesn't know how to live, to love, because she isn't safe. And the result is hate. When our hearts don't feel safe, we are threatened. When we are threatened, we lash out in hate.

But the good news is, the darkness is disappearing. There is light available. We just have to ask Jesus to bring it to those deepest places inside. He comes there, with perfect love, casting out fear, sometimes in stunning encounters, and usually little by little, day by day.

As our hearts feel safe in God's love, little by little, we get to rewrite the story, holding the brush alongside God as he begins to paint the page of restoration. We get to tell him how much we enjoy his company. We get to ask him to move the brush, just so. We get to reclaim what the traumatic and neglectful scenes tried to write into our lives. We get to allow something new to show up where the control and spirit of fear have reigned! We move from believing that we are, as the prophet Isaiah says, "The Forsaken City" or "The Desolate Land" and become those who believe we are the ones God delights in, "The Desirable Place" and "The City No Longer Forsaken" (Is. 62:3-5).

Sarah Bessey writes gloriously of what happened to her when she realized her heart was safe:

> I dug a new grave for my sarcasm and wicked anger, my self-defense and my own weak reputation, my "rights" and my pride, my comebacks and retaliations, then my need to be liked and understood and appreciated and approved. I prayed through every wound, every slight, every cruelty, every name-calling, every judgment, every hurt, and I released over and over again, *they know not what they do*. And I chose to make peace all over again. I chose ferocious gentleness. I chose kindness. I chose Love.[11]

I recognized this growing sense of safety in me one day while sorting through a sock drawer. What happened there has helped me know how I want to re-write the old story of control, allowing love to help me relax.

The cab was waiting outside, the driver doing crossword puzzles as he waited to take Steve to the airport for a flight to the Dominican Republic. Steve was running late and was rummaging through a few sock drawers with the look you get when you can't find that one last thing you need to pack in order to make your flight. Socks flew, and as they did I realized that he was looking for matching black socks and was finding only black, blue, dark blue, striped, dotted, thin, thick…nothing matching. Shame flooded my heart. For some old "Father Knows Best" reason, along with some legitimate desires to make Steve's life easier in all that he carries, I was horrified that I had not organized the socks before putting them in the drawer the last time laundry was done. I had shoved the socks in, a cacophony of blues, browns, black and whites.

I immediately felt the old familiar contempt rise up in my heart: "I am a terrible disappointment to him. I have failed. What is wrong with me?" Along with the contempt rose the fear: "He is furious with me. He is going to lash out at me any minute. I need to brace from the rage." Along with the fear rose the neglect, abandonment and spirit of fear: "He is done with me. He is going off on this trip so furious with me, and on this trip he will determine that the whole relationship is not worth it."

Crazy, isn't it?

With much joy I can report that I caught myself in this triggered moment. I felt the stiffness in my body and the Life of God rose in me to say, "What is this stiffness? Isn't that a bit extreme as you are simply watching a man look for socks?" I laughed inside. Then I heard myself. I heard the mocking, sarcastic, paranoid, extreme spirit of fear, and I caught myself. I wanted to defend myself, to lash out, to proclaim that I worked hard most of the time and I just didn't have time to clean the sock drawer. I was tempted to cower inside, to shamefully apologize, to skulk away in my self-contempt as he drove away.

But the Life of God won. I remembered the truth: Steve is a good man and he does not expect you to clean his sock drawer (he appreciates it, of course, but does not demand it nor require it). Steve is not your father, and you do not need to brace. Maybe, just maybe, he is not thinking dark thoughts about you in this moment. Maybe this moment has nothing to do with you! Maybe he is just frustrated with himself that he didn't pack sooner.

As I listened to this, the voice of Love, the Life of God, I settled down inside. I was quiet. I left his frantic searching and I went to go get a cup of coffee. Disaster averted. We kissed and he left on a sweet note. He was not upset with me in the least, and I smiled as I realized this. What could have been a contemptuous, heated or sullen moment became a moment of peace.

So don't fear, controlling sister. There's healing and change possible for you. You've sensed it; you know the kind of woman you want to be. Maybe—just maybe—you are loved more than you know. Maybe you are safe, after all. Maybe the beauty you suspected was in you still has a chance. How beautiful, when it seeps out of our shadows, is the inextinguishable light.

---

[9] Peter A. Levine, *Waking the Tiger: Healing Trauma* (Berkeley, CA: North Atlantic Books, 1997), 128.

[10] A 1997 study by the Michigan Child Protective Services found that 54% of victims in 1997 suffered neglect; 24%, physical abuse; 13%, sexual abuse; 6% emotional maltreatment; and 2%, medical neglect. Many children suffer more than one type of maltreatment.

[11] Sarahbessey.com, February 11, 2013.

Chapter Three
Pride: I Am Bitch, Hear Me Roar

Wrath plunders all the riches of the intellect, while the judgment remains the prisoner of its own pride.

~ Pietro Aretino

Been a whole lot easier since the bitch is gone / Little miss can't be wrong.

~ Spin Doctors

Your wisdom was corrupted by your love of splendor.

~ Ezekiel

Prideful Pangs

Pride is just ugly.

A woman I know carries a perpetual smug look on her face—the slight cock of her head, the crunch of her lips, the disdain that flashes through her eyes. It makes me sad when I feel this contortion of the face I enjoy. It makes her sad, too. If I catch her with that look, she can sense her arrogance immediately, but it is strong in her. Pride is ugly. It is what brought down the human race, after all.

Pride is the sister-sin of contempt. They are always in the same room, somehow. Pride can look like obvious rage, but it doesn't take rage to make us ugly. Sometimes we rage, and sometimes we simply raise an eyebrow.

Perhaps this subject scares you because you are afraid you have gone too far, lost too much kindness, said too much, destroyed too much along the way to ever be lovely again. Please know that there is hope. It has all been done before. Try to tell me of your glare as you shamed your husband sexually last week. Bring me your story of undercutting words or your attempts to block affection. Bring me the acid of your gossip, the haughty spirit of your religious activity. Tell me about your secret judgments and competition with another woman's body (or your hatred of your own). Try to convince me of the legitimacy of your hatred of yourself after your forays into pornography or sexual addiction. Bring to me your disdain for someone because of their politics or their parenting style. Bring me your hatred of the women who are married or the jealousy of the women who are single.

Every manifestation of pride or hateful treatment of ourselves or anyone else—especially those we love—has already been done.

Dante Alighieri said, "Avarice, envy, pride are the three fatal sparks, have set the hearts of all on fire."[12] When it comes to our relationships, pride is the fire that smolders until those caught-off-guard moments when it is exposed as an inferno. The smirk we carry, the disdain, the seething contempt—these are much more difficult to recognize than outright rage. But if we don't track down these insidious intruders to our beauty, soon they ignite a destructive fire.

Think of Elizabeth Bennett in Jane Austen's *Pride and Prejudice*, who said, "There are few people whom I really love, and still fewer of whom I think well. The more I see of the world, the more am I dissatisfied with it; and every day confirms my belief of the inconsistency of all human characters, and of the little dependence that can be placed on the appearance of either merit or sense."[13] Yikes. This is not just cynicism. Her potent, dismissive arrogance cuts others off at the knees. Is she hateful? Well, yes. But the smoldering fire of her sneering attitude consumes others with a slow burn more than an obvious hateful punch in the face. We similarly inflict mortal wounds to those we love with the rolling of our eyes.

Obviously this struggle is not relegated to us as women, but feminine pride has a sting all its own. This is a character issue, so we do well to not do too much narrative reflection until we have sat in the dust and ash of our destructive attitude. The fear of the Lord is the beginning of wisdom—I mean, it really is. We all know the proverb "pride comes before a fall," but we do well to hear the accompanying chorus around those words:

> Pride goes before destruction, and haughtiness before a fall. It is better to live humbly with the poor than to share plunder with the proud. Those who listen to instruction will prosper; those who trust the Lord will be happy. The wise are known for their understanding, and instruction is appreciated if it's well presented.... There is a path before each person that seems right, but it ends in death" (Prov. 16:18-25).

This is serious business.

We are all indicted. You may think you are the only one, but I promise you, you are not alone. In fact, if you recognize yourself in the definitions of pride above, that's good news—many women are blind to their own contempt. But the beauty of God is that we keep good company with the A-list of sinners in the Bible and beyond, and his love seems to have no trouble trumping their shame. As you might hear during a French Easter liturgy, "*L'amour de Dieu est folie!*" The love of God is folly! He is a fool for loving us when the biggest sneer on our face is pointed in his direction.

Shame and Contempt

Hosea, one of the more obscure prophets in the Old Testament, had the rare privilege of experiencing what God experiences every moment in relationship with our prideful, contemptuous selves. Old Testament prophets not only carried a message, but their lives *became* messages—meaning that the stories they were asked to live were to be for the people a picture of the heart of God. The bottom line is that Hosea was asked to love a woman who, because of the shame and self-contempt she felt, chose to heap prideful contempt on Hosea, viciously rejecting his advances and his love. If that is not an accurate picture of how it plays out with me and God, I don't know what is. There is lots of room for you and me in a story this wild.

Hosea is told to marry Gomer. Because Hosea's life was to be a picture of God's heart, immediately it becomes clear that Gomer is a picture of Israel's relationship with God—a relationship that had been perpetually broken by Israel in terms of every covenant instituted by God. Even before Hosea and Gomer existed, the betrayal of God's heart by his people was the one consistent theme in the whole story. God makes a way to have relationship, the people break it, and God forgives—that's the major theme of the story.

We are not told much about this woman Gomer except that she is a prostitute. Now, this is where things get a little dicey for me. Steve and I have the privilege of working alongside a handful of folks who work with women who are either trapped into the sex industry or compelled into prostitution due to poverty. These women would not choose to sell their bodies, but their circumstances have forced them into it. Elena and Sarai, who I mentioned previously, are good examples of this. Fantine in *Les Miserables* is also a perfect example of such a woman—she is a good woman, a precious woman, just trying to do well by her out-of-wedlock daughter, but who is so severely rejected for her immorality that she eventually has to sell her body.

In Gomer's case, on the surface it appears that she is not at all a victim, not at all exploited. In fact, on the surface it appears that Gomer is wantonly rebellious, running headlong after her customers. We don't know the circumstances of why she was selling her body, but if history is any indication, there had to have been some extenuating circumstances. We have to get up into the fabric of her life to discover the backstory to her brazen persona, because Gomer is a picture of me, you, and every other woman, exploited or otherwise.

Hosea does what God asks and marries Gomer, and over time he finds that he really loves this woman. But he has fallen in love with someone who continues to sell her body to others. That is how foolish the love of God is. The names given to the children Gomer bore while in prostitution are scathing, and they are telling of the severity of God's feelings about Israel's wandering heart. *Lo-ruhamah*, the name of one of her daughters, mean's "not loved." "For," says God, "I will no longer show love to the people of Israel or forgive them" (Hosea 1:6). The name of her son is *Lo-ammi*, which means "not my people."

Gomer is a picture of us. Eugene Peterson says that "listening to the prophets is like listening to a lover's quarrel through a bedroom wall." Well, this lover's quarrel has gotten really nasty, as happens when any lover's heart is betrayed and devastated. Hosea states firmly that if Gomer doesn't stop prostituting herself, "I will strip her naked. I will leave her to die of thirst, as in a desert or a dry and barren wilderness. And I will not love her children as I would my own because they are not my children! They were conceived in adultery. For their mother is a shameless prostitute and became pregnant in a shameful way" (Hosea 2: 1-4). Those are the words of a devastated lover.

Now, wait. I can hear you saying that this is *not* comforting to you as you contend with your own shame. But as I said, it has all done been done before. The way you display your arrogant independence, the "I know best" attitude, grieves the heart of God, but mostly because it is a betrayal of his trust. We can almost hear him saying, "Didn't you remember that I love you?" Our prodigal hearts keep good company with Gomer, who, after she had been shown the most lavish love by Hosea, pride-fully rebuffs him and contemptuously declares her independent superiority. She decides not only to return to prostitution, but also to go to her old customers with an offer to pay *them*, just to spite Hosea, the one who pursued her with smoldering love.

But w*hy* would Gomer stay in prostitution? Why would she harden so severely as to run after her old customers rather than melting into the love of man who pursues her with such grace? Again, what is behind her brazen, prideful contempt?

I suspect the answer is found, again, when we hear God's heart saying, "Did you not remember that I love you?" I suspect that what we are seeing with Gomer is exactly what plays out in us when we find ourselves full of contemptuous hatred.

Gomer felt ashamed. And it was Hosea's love that shamed her. It is impossible to share your body with others without experiencing shame, unless you dissociate. Gomer could have carried on in a semi-dissociative state of being, turning tricks and mindlessly going about her day, never really aware of the damage she was doing to herself. But then Hosea comes along and loves her. Now she is exposed. And now she is ashamed. Remember, that is what glory does: it exposes. That is what the kevod of God, the weighty nature of his love, does. I would imagine that when Hosea came into Gomer's life, she was already highly disconnected and shut down due to the shame she felt. Hosea walks into the life of a woman who feels deep shame, but who doesn't even realize her shame anymore. Hosea's love reminds her of the very thing she has shut down, the very thing she wants to forget. Hosea's love stirs the pot of her shame, and the result is a cauldron of contemptuous resistance.

But why the *contempt*?

Shame is a horrific experience. Jean Paul Sartre said that shame is "a hemorrhage of the soul." We will do anything to not experience it. When we feel that terrible feeling of being found lacking, when our humanity is exposed, we do what our father and mother Adam and Eve did—we hide. Generally our hiding takes the form of vicious contempt. Dan Allender says that contempt is the only force strong enough to match the intensity of shame. Contempt is our feeble attempt to trump the feeling of shame.

Well, Gomer truly did try to trump her shame. And you and I do the same. Of course it doesn't work; in fact, it usually makes matters worse. Gomer felt ashamed for her immorality, then felt doubly

ashamed for being a bitch to the man who is trying
to take care of her.

Thankfully, the focus of the whole story is that
Hosea never relented in his pursuit. And God never
relents in his pursuit of us, despite the hateful
gymnastics we do to try to hide. He'll find myriad
ways to trip us up in our sneering hatred as we try
to cover over our perceived deficiencies; as we try
to hide in our destructive pride and self-sufficiency.
He says:

> I will fence her in with thornbushes, I
> will block the road to make her lose
> her way. When she runs after her
> lovers, she won't be able to catch up
> with them. She will search for them
> but not find them. Then she will think,
> "I might as well return to my husband,
> because I was better off with him than
> I am now". She doesn't realize that it
> was I who gave her everything she
> has—the grain, the wine, the olive oil"
> (Hosea 2: 6-8).

Yes, we keep good company with Gomer – both
in her shame and in God's foolish grace.

Prodigal Hearts

I've always been struck with the phrase we just
heard from Gomer, "I might as well return." When
Jesus taught about the kingdom of God being like the
story of the prodigal son, the essence of that phrase—

"I might as well"—was repeated by the son after he had spent his inheritance.: "When he finally came to his senses, he said to himself, 'At home even the hired servants have food enough to spare, and here I am dying of hunger! I will go home to my father and say, "Father, I have sinned against both heaven and you, and I am no longer worthy of being called your son. Please take me on as a hired servant." "(Luke 15:19-21). Can you hear the "I might as well" attitude in this? The prodigal was not yearning to go home; he just figured it would be better than the mess he was in. Gomer did not really want to respond to Hosea's love—she didn't want to be exposed, remember—but she figured she might as well.

Yes, we keep good company with Gomer, and we keep good company with the prodigal who, in his prideful, sneering contempt, decided he knew best and took his inheritance to a far-off country for sex tourism, rampant homosexual and heterosexual orgies, gambling, days of binging and purging, slothful sleeping, and drug experimentation until he just couldn't take it anymore. It wasn't that he wanted to go home; he just resigned himself that "it would be better for me there than here."

We keep good company with every other prodigal female who got caught looking the other way on their stumble home, only to be caught off guard by a robe, a ring, and an all-out party. We can barely feel the soil of home beneath our feet for the gentle pulsing of the drumbeat, can barely smell the stench of our independence for the wafting of grilled meats, extravagant spices and the inexplicable aroma of merriment, this party on our behalf. Our pride is trumped by the hilarity of God, and our contempt trumped by kindness. Beauty will win if we can be caught off guard by Jesus, who celebrates us even though we don't trust him.

How Our Stories Make Us Prideful

If we reach that point, the point of being amazed at the restorative, hilarious, illogical embrace of God, then we can look again at our stories. Remember, we do so because it helps; it helps us to understand why we were so foolish in the first place. It helps us understand the particularity of the healing that we need.

If you listen carefully to your story, searching for the birthplace of pride, you are likely to find a scene in which you were powerful or had an impact (especially if your world generally told you otherwise). Sadly the scene often involves some sort of shame, a shadow out of which we grab hold of the lifeline of power and pride, some sense that we were imperative, needed, or desired. You may have felt prized only to find it evaporated or was used selfishly. As a result of our stories, we cherish our power and despise it at the same time.

Here is more of my story, which I share gingerly, to flesh out an example of the moments when a seed of pride is planted. I actually wrote this portion of my story several years ago, before my mother died. I wanted her to read my recollection of events, which we had spoken of together, but which had never been written. She granted me permission for this story to be shared, and her words were, "If it will help anyone else, please share it, honey. It is a sad story. But I am most sad about how I hurt you." That was the beauty in my mother's heart, always a resounding solid melody line underneath cacophonous harmonies.

Once again, as you read, listen for the ways I discovered I was powerful, that I had an impact:

* * * * *

The couch was long, longer than most, furniture designed to fit nicely in a Santa Fe portico, but it consumed our small living room. My mother sat, stone-faced, on one end of this couch. I had come tromping in from an unusually good day at school—sixth grade was proving to be better than I had hoped, mostly due to the kindness of my teacher, Mrs. Schelonka. I took the back way home, through pinion and cactus laden trails and across a few choice arroyos. The September sun continued to hold its warmth in the afternoon hours, so I was slightly sweaty when I climbed the driveway.

As I came through the door, I caught a glimpse of mom's face. The moment I had learned to fear was happening again. On the long couch, it was happening again.

I was being beckoned, without a word.

I felt a simultaneous revulsion and thrill. I knew my plan to hang out in my room with the radio was now interrupted, but a thrill—an *honor*—rose up in

me. I felt called into something for which I was
becoming well practiced, but it scared me. I wanted
so much to come up with what was necessary to
address whatever madness might come. I felt a slight
nausea, the kind you get when you know you are
heading into danger. I thought, *Can I do it?* but I
pushed down this revulsion, made it behave, as I had
many times before, and summoned a strength never
intended for a child.

Something about this moment seemed urgent. I
stepped near the couch; I saw a different hue on
mom's face, a mysterious look my twelve-year-old
eyes had not yet witnessed. I was about to be
beckoned into a new world, a world I should have
been sheltered from at all costs. But instead, I looked
in mom's eyes and saw only pleading, girlish pain.

"He was so kind," she said. "It was his way of
showing love. He didn't know any other way of
showing love." Mom had become an eight-year-old in
my presence, barely maintaining an adult tone. Her
feigned maturity broke my heart, and I knew I now
was a twelve-year-old listening to an eight-year-old.
Maybe I could help after all.

Mom began to weep. Then she began to convulse.
I held her, as I had so many times before. The honor
and thrill set in. *I am helping.* The revulsion rising. *I
am lost.* Deep sobs came from her tiny frame. "Mom,
what is it? Mom, what is it? What happened?"

The words came tumbling out of Mom's mouth,
but my imagination was the only bridge to her words.
She told of a man who took care of her in the Kansas

summers after her mother had died, when her own father was away on business. She spoke of this man's sexual requests of her beginning at age eight, until she was fifteen. As my mother told the story, she looked at me, pleading for help. I felt frigid inside but did not dare show it. I feebly wondered: *What do you want from me?*

* * * * *

My child's heart was hemorrhaging as I was drawn into her ambivalent despair. But because I was being entrusted with something, it was a privilege. There was an adultness to my determination to navigate, to know how to help, to find the fruit of understanding which, in the distant wisdom of Eden, was relegated to a forbidden, protective tree.

I was suddenly powerful, but it was no power I would ever wish for myself. Earlier years of abandonment set my heart up to be so thrilled that I would be invited in. She had grown to need me, and I found I could make her feel better just by being there. I felt intense shame over not being able to understand or comprehend what she was saying, what was happening. This whole convoluted scene was, in many ways, the birthplace of intense pride.

I was chosen, I was needed, and I figured out how to navigate my way through this adult neediness. The sad reality is that I was really good at it, skilled at calming her down, comforting her—until I was brought too far into my mom's own dissociative recollection of abuse. Evil was waiting there (as it always is, in the wings with a hurting child), taunting me with pressured pride, *You are very good at what you do, Jan, but you had better find a way to be ready at all times to come through, even if you don't know what you are doing.*

Our False Interpreter

It was a taunt that brought with it an *interpretation of my world.* Remember, that's what evil does in our greatest moments of harm—it comes to us with a translation, an interpretation that helps us make sense of our world, when no one else is interpreting anything for us. Evil's interpretation was, "Don't you see? You exist to be helpful. So you better find a keep that up or you'll find yourself alone." Then evil makes an offer to us, almost like a shield for our trembling heart: "If you find a way, I will help you. You can do it (without God). You can do it (without God)." My young heart said yes, because it did not know what else to do. I found a way to be helpful. Thomas Jefferson wisely said that pride costs us more than hunger, thirst, or cold. The cost for me was my vulnerable tenderness, my confession that of course I did not know how to help in such graphic circumstances. I grabbed hold of the offer (which is never fully a conscious choice, especially when we are young). I found a way.

Somewhere along the way, this interpretation and the way I (unwittingly) said yes to it, made me into a fiercely self-sufficient woman. Oh, people thought of me as nice. I was the helpful girl, voted "best personality" in my senior class. But my motivation was self-sufficiency, and I developed a deeper arrogant smirk for how well I loved and how helpful I would always be.

Jesus invites us to a grace we did not even know we needed. At certain times, this invitation rides in a soft wind toward us, wafting past our consciousness with a plea. At other times it firmly speaks, clear, definitive in its exposing voice:

> *What has convinced you that your own resources are best for the pain and confusion? What convinced you that you could hold back the tide of all that is unmanageable in your world? Do you see who you are becoming? You are rigid, tight, braced, and angry. There's more to you than this, if you'll trust me to care for you and to give you what you need. Admit that you do not see clearly. You were never meant to see clearly! It is a weight that will crush you, and it did crush you when you were young, being asked to know too much. Come rest while I take care of it all, for I alone know.*

The Knowledge of Good and Evil

I have learned that there's no way, even with evil's offer to help, that I can ever navigate the complexities of anyone's harm, let alone their hearts, on my own, in my own knowledge. When I do rely on my own knowledge, I am not a woman or a counselor you want to be with. But when I relinquish my ability and lean in to the stunning wisdom and knowledge of Jesus, I find that he is beautifully skillfully helpful— and I find that I am, too. But the pressure is no longer on me. I no longer have to be a prideful bitch, determined to prove I am skilled and helpful, so I don't sink into the elephant mud of this terribly sad world. No, I get to show up, ride along, and watch Jesus heal people. And it is just much more fun.

There were two trees, after all. Actually, I think we should say there *are* two trees, the tree of knowledge of good and evil and the tree of life. They show up in countless fables, fairy tales, and legends as heroes and heroines are tempted to know *all,* tempted to hold knowledge of what is good and evil—to hold the very intelligence of God. When the serpent came and spun its tale, it played with the notion—it interpreted—that God was deceiving Eve, that he was withholding good things from her by asking her to refrain from knowing that which only God was meant to know.

And then comes my least favorite line in the scriptures: "Eve was convinced."

She was convinced that God was keeping from her even more beauty and stunning life than she and Adam had enjoyed up to that point. Even in a garden, a beautiful place unsullied by *anything.*

I took it slow today, and wandered my garden between projects. I watered a bit around 8:00 a.m.

and took note of how much the hibiscus has recovered since a hard Colorado hail stripped it a month ago. I saw the color slowly returning to the long veins of the purple sage, and saw the Shasta daisies starting to open, Soon they will dance. Then I stared at the clematis, which had not fared so well—it had a certain shredded quality to it. I found my mind jumping from my own weary garden to the breathtaking, sculpted beauty of the gardens of London or Tokyo, then to the rain forest around Victoria Falls and the tropical jungles along the Amazon basin, to the vivid color on the wings of birds in Ethiopia—all thought up in the hilarious playground of God's heart.

Then my mind wandered to Eve's garden. *What in the world?* I could not believe what I imagined.

I saw a verdant, expansive place, with lots of room to explore. It was filled with unnamed colors, like the aquamarine off the coast of Sri Lanka, the turquoise of the water off of Kauai, the purple hue of dusk over the Sangre de Cristo Mountains, the amber on the plains above Cape Town—only *better.* The scents were pungent, but never overwhelming. They were something like the high desert of Northern New Mexico after a summer rain, the lilting surprise of Spring dogwood, a crush of fresh heather—only *better.* The air, well…there's no describing its purity, or the sheer health felt when taking a deep, long breath. The sounds were sounds of love. That was the backdrop.

The best part was seeing Eve's face. She was so...happy. So completely at rest. The waters ran in cadence with the inner chambers of her heart. She and Adam explored the sands and lush grass, wandered along a windy mountain stream. Every day was different, but every day found him exploring her—her personality, her way, her thoughts, her body—without shame. Every day she allowed that exploration, loved it, and reciprocated, all without a shadow of contempt. They had the spacious freedom to wonder about each other, to inquire without time constraints or the fear of being misunderstood. They could make love timelessly without fear or dread for how the wounds of the past might take from them. And what partners they were!

They were told to go out together to make this beautiful place even more beautiful. They were artisans with carnelian, onyx, pearl, diamonds, with cedar and acacia and walnut and pine. The light from their Father's heart wove its way into every aspect of their world—translucent, shimmering, bearing perfect peace and warmth.

I looked back at my struggling, shredded clematis and compared them to Eden's tumbling acres of stunning blossoming vines. The distance between the two is, well, just so *far*.

But I can imagine it. We all can. Something in us knows. While it is true that "no eye has seen, no ear has heard, and it has not entered into the heart of man, the things being prepared for us" (I Cor. 2:9), we have already imagined Eden. We were created for it; we carry it in our DNA. We know it like we know the tendency of our great grandfather toward shag carpet and cigarette smoke, or the legacy of our mother's brilliant acuity with crossword puzzles. Our genetic heritage comes seeping out—we may have never visited, but our hearts have rehearsed the stories of our homeland countless times without even realizing it. Even if we live in the heart of the city, or have a life dedicated to the slums, our hearts are beckoned back to Eden beauty even by a lonely butterfly landing on a trashcan.

But even there, Eve was convinced that God was withholding something from her. I like how Francis Shaeffer puts it: "The Fall was from a very high place." Even that high, lovely place was not enough to hold her heart, to keep her heart from being suspicious of God's heart toward her. She wanted the comfort of the certainty that comes from being in charge.

So when the serpent came, bearing spin on the instructions God had given Adam, Eve started to wonder if there might be even *more* that God was keeping from her. Evil's spin brought an idea she liked; she could rest in her own ability to know the things of God, she could check up on him so she would not have to live in the tension of trusting his care and provision and knowledge of her. Eve believed, she was taken in, with the notion that there was more to know, it was being withheld from her, and she should be privy to it. Thus the essence of our foolish beliefs: God cannot be trusted. He's seems good but he in fact has dark intentions. Suspicion is needed. We should use caution when interacting with God.

Eve did not need healing; she needed a rescue from her fearful unbelief. She believed the only goodness she could trust—the only source she could depend on—was her own ability to know, see, and control. Her fear led to control. Her control led to prideful contempt.

There's an alternative, and we can eat of it—the tree of life—anytime. The life that allows our hearts to say, *I don't have to have the full story. I'm safe here. There are things I was not meant to fully understand. I will leave it all in the hands of God, because I can trust that He has my best in mind, even if I can't see it.*

Life is found in dependent trust.

Tongues of Bitches

I remember the first time I held and meditated on a scripture. It was a simple phrase, "A gentle answer turns away wrath"(Prov. 15:1).[14] My brother had given me *The Jesus Person Pocket Promise Book*. That little book was a treasure in the heart of a young teenager trying to navigate the craziness you have been hearing about. The words held life for me— became my intention, yes, gave me the resolve I needed to hold my own tongue when I was becoming too practiced at raging at dad, trading rage for rage. It held me together, helped me know I could have gentle answers when my father was intractable in his anger. It calmed me down.

By the time I was fifteen, I had developed articulate ways of defending myself. As the book of James says, "The tongue is a small thing that makes grand speeches." I was learning how to duck and cover under words, sometimes brilliantly, as a means of deflecting any chance of being shamed, ignored, or harmed. As James goes on to say, "But a tiny spark can set a great forest on fire. And the tongue is a flame of fire. It is a whole world of wickedness, corrupting your entire body. It can set your whole life on fire, for it is set on fire by hell itself" (James 3:5,6).[15] I wielded this weapon of self-protection at times with savvy, and at times with irrational raging words.

As Jesus has been taking me deeper into realms of his love, my tongue has been losing its bite. But Steve, because he has that privilege of loving me for better or worse, still often pays the price for my combat mode with my father. There are some proverbs that just pack a punch, like: "Every wise woman builds her house, but the foolish one *tears it down with her own hands*" (Prov. 14:1).[16] This proverb sends a chill of warning down my spine. It should. The problem is, again, that our foolish words often come tumbling out in triggered moments.

This happened last night. Steve was on the phone with one of our grown daughters (my step-daughters, who I cherish). He was making plans with her for something the next day. I had told him that morning I was weary, that I needed a break from all activity for a few days. It was a deep need, and I had stated my need respectfully and he had responded with love, compassion and reassurance that he would do everything in his power to protect my time.

When I heard him making plans, though, I was triggered by the old abandonment wound, and the Spirit of Fear showed up. Suddenly my world was spinning. I felt like an ocean was covering my ability to breathe. In that moment, I was not curious about the context of the conversation; I did not want to hear the back-story, a story of how Steve was making plans in a way that did honor a desire to protect me. No, I was in an irrational fight for my life, convinced I was being forgotten, neglected, and overlooked. Internally, I was the terrified child, and something rose up to defend her. I was bitterly accusing of Steve. I glared at him while he was on the phone, and sarcastically attacked him verbally when he got off the phone: "I *knew* you would not protect me. Thanks a *lot* for making plans when you promised. Everyone else is more important to you than me." Ouch. Even as I write that I cringe at the level of abusive, accusatory cruelty that can come out of abandonment wounds. I did not realize that Steve had made every effort to protect me, even as he made his own plans. It had not crossed my mind that I would be honored, remembered.

My words are not always biting, but my wound is a chronic wound. Foolishness is always just a trigger away, jolting the bitch from her sleep. Friedrich Nietzsche spoke of the actual physiological effect on someone in the presence of that kind of ugliness. He said, "It weakens and afflicts man. It recalls decay, danger, impotence; he actually suffers a loss of energy in its presence." (I can see the life drain from Steve's face when he experiences my rage.) Nietzsche goes on to say, "The effect of the ugly can be measured with a dynamometer. Whenever man feels in any way depressed, he senses the proximity of something ugly. His feeling of power, his will to power, his courage, his pride—they decline with the ugly, they increase with the beautiful."

Heaven help us.

Love: The Antidote to Pride

Chronic wounds require daily healing. Once we recognize they are there, it really is a matter of holding that place inside open to Jesus, for him to come to it, for it, in whatever way he determines. It is not a formula—on the contrary, Jesus is always disarming. His conviction can be quite strong before this occurs, for we have to see our bitch and grieve the damage she does. "Godly sorrow leads to repentance," the Apostle Paul says. Notice he did not say, "Being disgusted with yourself leads to repentance." No, it is pure conviction and simply being sorrowful, not having an answer for what we have done, no excuses.

That is the first step in healing.

Then we search for the unhealed places in our story, and once we find them, we then get to ask for something from him: "Jesus, come and heal this place in me that I cannot reach. It is hurting, lacking, scared, unsafe. Come make it safe, so I do not need to rage."

He will—not always right away, and never in the way we imagined he would. But he will.

As I sat to write this book today, I felt a nagging shame, a low-grade accusation that the residue from the ugly in my life was blocking what the book could be. I decided to turn on Yo Yo Ma's rendition of Gabriel's Oboe, to help center my thoughts and heart on Jesus' love for me rather than my shame, to let his morning light wash over me at the kitchen table. I love his light.

Well, I was caught off guard completely. As I basked in the glory of the magnificent strings of that score, I told Jesus that I wanted to create something beautiful for him, to please him. He immediately took me to the time when I was eight years old. I had just drawn a picture, and I could not wait to show it to someone. Jesus stepped right into the scene. He said, "Do you see my expression?" I did—his face was so excited, his demeanor warm, lit up, thrilled! He was so aware of my little heart and all the beauty it wanted to capture in the creating. Because of this, my heart was, well…thrilled in response. It was so fun. I couldn't wait to draw another picture.

Then, Jesus carefully stepped aside and asked me to contrast his response with the response in my home. (Please remember, it was Jesus who was doing this. I was not forcing these thoughts). I looked again at Jesus' delighted face, and then looked around to see my dad glance at my drawing. He smiled, said it was good, and he even enjoyed looking at it. But the moment was very brief, and he went back to his crossword puzzle. His gaze was gone. I turned to my mom, and her response was one of delight, "It is so pretty, honey." Her response warmed me, but it wasn't enough.

I could see what Jesus was after. He wanted me to see the depth of my longing. How deeply it is set in me to create something that is pleasing. I could see he was showing, again, that his delighted gaze was the only safe place for that longing.

The core message I walked away with from this disarming encounter was this: *You are safe, and you don't have to know how to handle anything except being delighted in. You don't have to know everything, you don't have to handle anything. It is okay to simply want to create something stunning. I'll love it even if it is full of mistakes. I see it; I see you. Relax.* He winked at me. What an unbelievably wise and kind Father. The Trinity showed up all at one time. The Spirit took me to Jesus, who revealed to me the Father's heart. So fun. So beautiful.

You've been awful, and you've presumed all kinds of wickedness about God, just as I have. He winks at you. Just as your hand reaches for the tree of the knowledge of good and evil, and you snarl back when someone offers you some feedback…just as you reject the tree of life, seething that your whole community will be in error if your opinion is not listened to…here he is, throwing a party for you. Just as a torrent of shame washes your forehead as you recognize your arrogant betrayal of his kindness, he comes with a soft, white robe to cover you.

You might as well relax and get used to your humanity, admit your wandering, catch yourself sneering. Take the fruit of life and find him. Or take the deceptive fruit and *find him still*, prodigal sister. He won't leave you, even in your most arrogant suspicion of him.

---

[12] Dante Alighieri, *The Divine Comedy* (New York, NY: Oxford University Press, 2003), "Hell" Canto VI.

[13] Jane Austen, *Pride and Prejudice* (Rockville, MD: Manor, 2008), 29.

Chapter Four

Desire: The Audacity of Addiction

I wish the days to be as centuries, loaded, fragrant.
~ R.W. Emerson
You are pulled from the wreckage of your silent reverie.
~ Sarah McLaughlin
Give us that bread every day of our lives.
~ John 6

The War of Desire

The bitch inside us is at war with her desire.

Our problem is not that we don't wrangle with our bad desires. No, the problem is: we don't articulate clearly enough for ourselves, and to God, what it is we truly want. When we ignore our desire our lives go haywire or we shut down. It actually takes a ton of energy to ignore our longings, but we do find a way to ignore, shame, or kill our desire, and when we do, it has a name: addiction.

Some of us are stiff and controlling, some are sneering and contemptuous, and some of us have simply disappeared. Our presence has left the room. And when we disappear, it puts us at great risk for addiction. We've already talked about how much tension there is in this beautiful already-but-not-yet world of ours. A tension-filled, disappointing world is rife with addiction. This world, as I say in *The Allure of Hope*, is:

...the perfect place for getting fat, having an affair, getting more parts of your body pierced, getting skinny, trying cocaine, maxing out a credit card, pouring yourself into ministry, devouring romance novels, developing networks of gossip .... Why? Because there's nothing else to do? No, because we are running from desire. C.S. Lewis said the problem with most Christians is that they don't want enough. Again, how can that be? How can it be that I want too little when I feel wanton and frivolous for wanting the things I do want? But if we are honest, we can easily see the truth in Lewis's familiar words: "We are half-hearted creatures, fooling about with drink and sex and ambition when infinite joy is offered us, like an ignorant child who wants to go on making mud pies in a slum because he cannot imagine what is meant by the offer of a holiday at the sea. We are far too easily pleased."[14]

We kill desire by finding M&Ms and consuming forty of them without really tasting one. We shut down our hearts by downing an entire six-pack of microbrew alone, rather than enjoying one or two bottles slowly, with a friend, over an honest conversation. We take flight into an obsessive relationship, believing that without the person's presence or affirmation, we will die. We hoard a man's compliments like a secret stash of manna. We appear free of addiction but are steeped in it as we have a long conversation over lunch with a friend— the entire time discussing another woman's marriage "out of concern for her." A gossip addiction, sanctified. We turn our face from our true desire and find a few solitary hours with porn—either actual websites or three of the latest *InStyle* or *Vogue* or, even better, *Men's Health* magazines. Rather than trying on a new outfit and purchasing but one piece of the ensemble—dreaming of the time we can complete the package—max out the credit card and buy all the new styles of the season at once. We commit ourselves to three volunteer activities when we really only have a heart for one, and might not even have time for that. We watch *The Bachelor*—or read through a morning liturgy—mindlessly.

Most women I know are too busy to even fantasize about having an affair, but the overextended calendar can serve a similar purpose. Goodness, often it *is* an affair, a tryst with adrenalin or work. Women in middle management are a growing segment of our population, as we try to break the glass ceiling. Sometimes the drive to success is truly out of necessity to provide, but sometimes we fight an enemy that isn't even there. Often our successes come from a detached willingness to carry a weight far too big for our shoulders, especially when carried along with the management of a home and family. Same can be said for how often we dive into too much church activity, to feel the strokes from a church culture which lauds overextended women.

Staying Alive to Desire

Madeleine L'Engle wrote, "When we were children, we used to think that when we were grown-up we would no longer be vulnerable. But to grow up is to accept vulnerability. . . . To be alive is to be vulnerable."[15]

Leaving our addictions means we will feel naked. It feels crazy to give up our addictive covers, especially those the bitch inside of us holds on to with bleeding fingernails. But our forays into anything that numbs or overindulges are attempts to mitigate our ache, to create for ourselves a space where there is no disappointment, loss, or aloneness. We refuse to bend under the weight of the fall, and feel, along with Eve, "you will have an unmet aloneness in every arena of giving life, and you will have a fierce demand to be certain of your husband's desire for you, and way with you, but you will be disappointed and as he is his own person" (my paraphrase of Gen 3:14-16). *Oh, no—we will not suffer like Eve*, we say. Our addictions are our attempt to rise above the fall, to answer the dilemma ourselves. Rather than admit our vulnerability in our loneliness and our lack of control, rather than allow the fall to draw our hearts to our true safety in the heart of God, we refuse and create our own shield of defense.

Now, before this is misinterpreted as too complimentarian, conservative, or old school, please know I could write a parallel paragraph about Adam. He would do anything to avoid the futility of life, or the shame of exposure, so he grabs the fig leaf of competence or blame shifting. It isn't that our heritage with Eve carries any more misaligned power than a man's heritage with Adam. We both have to learn to bend, humble ourselves, and admit our need. Our needs just look different, that's all—at least a smidgen, but that smidgen is significant. And therefore our addictions tend to have a male/female flavor to them.

If you scan through your addictive tendencies, I am guessing they have a relational ache at their core. If a man does the same, there is likely a longing for impact at the core. For both men and women, our addictions create a world where we don't have to ask, seek or knock; we don't have to come with a child's heart and desire; we don't have to wait; we don't have to suffer. Women tend to suffer just a bit more in the loneliness department; men tend to suffer a bit more as they feel the impact of futility and pressure. These are not static, rigid categories, but they are fluid realities I have seen fleshed out in my work with people across cultures.

There is great power in casting off our respective fig leaves. Sounds downright arousing, doesn't it? Actually, it is quite sensual, because it allows us to receive God's covering of our shame, and then the power to love. I love how Sarah Bessey puts it: "We submit to each other and because we follow Him, we both practice playing second fiddle." Vulnerability and mutual submission are great—albeit risky— aphrodisiacs.

By way of contrast, in the world of addiction, we create reality as we want it. We are tempted to say that it doesn't work, but the reality is, most addictions are effective for a while. If you don't want to feel the longing for motherhood when you've been trying to get pregnant for months, chronic TV watching will work for a while to get you out of the dilemma of desire. If you are weary of hoping for the job you really want, several fast food stops is a great help. If you are longing for a deeper relationship with your daughter and she is intractable, there are plenty of prescription drugs available through the internet to assuage the ache. But most importantly, if you don't want the energy of real love to be stirred in you, choose your addiction du jour—it is a sure passion killer.

But the helpers don't really help, of course, over the long haul. The fig leaves cover nothing. We build a house of cards, a shelter of our own making, thinking it is big enough to crawl under to be safe. God speaks in a comically incredulous way about this in the Prophets when he says, "You have no place of refuge–the bed you have made is too short to lie on. The blankets are too narrow to cover you" (Isaiah 28:20). What we try to do in our emotional gymnastics to create another world for ourselves isn't just silly, it is dishonest. Dan Allender says that this is an attempt "to become as God with the power to construct the world and reality according to our desire."[16] We become slaves to our own selfish idols, but we don't even see that we are in chains.

This Is Your Brain on Desire

Now, I want to be careful here, because there are strong physiological components to our addictions that compound our war with desire. Usually our addictions are a delicate balance of both a flight from desire (and the pain of unmet desire) and chemical and neurological relief that comes from whatever activity or substance we choose. Over 25% of search engine requests are for pornography—over 68 million requests a day—and the majority of those occur between 9:00am and 5:00pm on business computers. If this is an indication that hearts are yearning for something (and it is), then it is also an indication that the neurochemicals released during porn viewing have hooked more of our friends than we know. It takes more than a desire to view sex to risk your employment or your marriage—that kind of risky behavior flows from adrenalin gone mad, a literal physiological addiction to the thrill imbedded in visual and sexual stimulation.

Last spring I fell while cleaning high interior windows (I know, I know, no lectures please). The full weight of my body crashed into the corner of a heavy, solid wooden coffee table, breaking five ribs, two in two places. These were not fractures; they were breaks. It is impossible to describe the pain of broken ribs. All I can say is: rest your hands on your ribcage. Now breathe. The ribs move with every breath. Every. Breath. There is nothing to be done. Ribs cannot be braced or casted or bound due to risk of pneumonia. You must sleep sitting up. And painkillers—hefty ones—are imperative. I was on strong pain medication for six weeks, lower levels for eight weeks. I was on dilaudid and oxycontin for the first four weeks, then on oxycodone for the remaining weeks. These pills are opiates—heroin in a little orange bottle with a script attached.

This experience gave me much compassion for those who are chronically addicted to opiates, because the process of coming off those pills was brutal—terrifying, actually. My body had developed a new threshold of normal, so normal became the angelic state of being these opiates provide. If you know the song "In the Arms of an Angel" by Sarah McLachlan, it speaks lyrically about the power of heroin, but the song also *feels* like the state of being that opiates bring. Even as I write this, I crave it. David Wilcox sings, "A poppy flower is beautiful; a thousand poppies is dangerous." Sometimes we are in danger without realizing it.

Even though my struggle to come off the drugs was physiological, and I was thankfully able to extricate myself from those glorious and tormenting pills in reasonable time, my experience captures the overarching dynamics of addiction. The opiates created a pain-free existence for me, and I came to really love that altered state. The pills took away the ripping pain in my ribs, but they also eased and decompressed my mind when it came to things I didn't even realize were affecting me: worry about the details of launching a new business (which Steve was doing); stress over my aging father's assisted living needs; the fragile state of several of my counseling clients. All this happened over the span of eight weeks, and I did not even realize it. I was in denial about the potent impact of the drugs, and in denial about how much I had come to relish their assistance.

Denial of Desire

Ah yes, our addictions are saturated in denial. We're all familiar with the term. It's the first thing an alcoholic or drug addict has to face before anything can change, right? We have to get out of denial and face our destructive ways. We've watched Dr. Phil or Dr. Drew, so we get the reason why sometimes an intervention is necessary—it is a time to come face to face with what we are doing to those we love.

But denial is not only blindness to our impact on others, refusal to see physiological dependency, or the energy we put into creating a safe world. I come back to my original point: we deny the specific longings that we are trying to outrun.

I love how Winn Collier puts it:

> Whenever I ask someone Jesus' question: What do you want?, I often receive an anticipated litany that you'd find in any respectable Sunday School

curriculum. The answers are fine, but they often possess all the verve of a dead fish. I want the real stuff, what makes the heart race and the energy peak and the sorrow sit heavy as lead.

Often, it would be more truthful if we said: I really want my wife to enjoy sex with me again or I want to stop puking in the toilet or I want money so I can fly the family to Italy for the summer or I want the voices to stop. These would all be closer to the truth. If it's true that what we really want is to land on the *Times* bestseller list or to be kissed like mad, why don't we say so?"[17]

Bingo. He is so right, isn't he? But speaking like this makes us more than nervous. It feels like madness to remind ourselves of things we don't have and may never have. C.S. Lewis speaks of this conversation as having the power to open an "inconsolable longing."[18] Oh, I know what you are thinking—some of the things on your wish list seem downright immature, selfish, and ludicrous. Maybe. But we have to dig through that dirt to get to the gold—the thirst for exploration, relationship, intimacy, giving life, offering beauty, creativity, strength, and being enjoyed. Our hearts long for things we rarely entertain.

Just think about the last time you headed out of town on a camping trip, just as early morning light hit your windshield. You can't tell me you didn't feel giddy, that it didn't prick an entire ocean of adventure lust within you. Well, that ocean, along with the ocean of desire to be beautiful, to have an impact on your world, to be inspirational, runs deep in you. Go ahead and try to dry it up. It can't be done. Go ahead and try to kill your desires by indulging or anesthetizing. The desire is in you, so you are going to have to do *something* with it. Killing it completely doesn't work.

Choosing a Deeper Desire

You have to become an honest dreamer in order to have an honest thirst for God. Sometimes you have to take a bite of an appetizer in order to realize how famished you are. Sometime you have to take a sip in order to understand how real your actual thirst is.

I can hike for miles without taking a single drink from my Nalgene bottle. But the moment I stop and take a drink, I am parched. I was parched three miles back on the trail, but I just did not realize it. The point is: dream about the safari in Africa so you can recognize how much you were crafted for constant adventure; desire deeply to have children for whom to make pancakes so you can remember how fully you were created to give life, in any form; dream big about the promotion, because you crave to embody the glory of God.

Will you get sullen if you don't vacation this year?
Bewildered if you don't get pregnant? Will you get
obsessive about your job? Maybe. But at least you will
be alive, as well as face to face with what it is that
holds your affection. Those dreams—they matter! But
they just can't provide life. Sometimes you just have
to realize you are thirsty for even more than the best
your mind can imagine. The beauty in this process,
albeit risky, is that though the outcome of the things
we dream about is not within our control, the deeper
things of God, the deeper beauty, is constant. As Pope
John Paul II says:

> It is Jesus that you seek when you
> dream of happiness; He is waiting for
> you when nothing else you find
> satisfies you; He is the beauty to which
> you are so attracted; it is He who
> provoked you with that thirst for
> fullness that will not let you settle for
> compromise; it is He who urges you to
> shed the masks of a false life.[19]

Jesus and a man were once discussing this very
thing. The man wanted a miracle like manna,
something he could be sure of. But Jesus knew he
didn't want *enough*. Jesus said, "Moses didn't give
bread from heaven. My father did. Now he offers you
the true bread from heaven. The true bread of God is
the one who comes down from heaven and gives life
to the world." The man said the smartest thing any of

us could ever say: "Sir, give us that bread every day of our lives." Jesus is the dream we really want, anyway.

God wants your heart. The bitch wants you protected. God is not concerned that you clean up your lavish spending habits or binging in secret as much as he longs for you to bring to him your tender ache, confusion, and pain over your unmet desires. The bitch will make sure you never let the tender ache surface. Obviously, there is no guarantee about the outcome of dreaming—if I told you there was a guarantee, you would hate me. That's why we have such dismissive contempt for infomercials. But the bitch sneers at our desperate longing and mocks it, calling it weak and foolish. I like how Sharon Hersh articulates it: "Redemption does not mean that God meets our needs and then our souls stop longing. No, redemption does not eradicate desperation. Instead, redemption allows us to surrender." What are we surrendering? We are surrendering our self-crafted, personal attempts to alter our reality. We are letting go of calling the shots. We are asking the bitch to step aside, telling her we understand why she is so scared, hurt and angry, but that her services of self-protection are no longer needed. We open our grip and allow both desire and the suffering from unmet desire to be real. Sharon goes on to say, "We don't give up craving. We give in to craving God. And God doesn't want something from us. He wants us."[20]

Don't you love it when you are preferred over someone or something, when a friend chooses to spend time with you rather than a movie they had planned, or when your partner makes it clear that they would rather be with you than golfing? Gerald May says this, similarly, about our desires:

> If our choice of God is to be made with integrity we must first have felt other attractions and chosen, painfully, not to make them our gods. True love, then, is not only born of freedom; it is also born of difficult choice. A mature and meaningful love must say something like, "I have experienced other goodnesses, and they are beautiful, but it is You, my true heart's desire, whom I choose above all."[21]

It is dangerous to speak this way. I know all too well. I longed for marriage through many lonely seasons. My life was rich and full, but if I had been successful in shutting down that desire (and I succeeded for a while at times, for sure), I am positive I would not have had much to offer as a woman to my clients, my community. I would not have had much to offer as a writer. I'm positive I would not have enjoyed the riches of my life. The desire was deep, and I had to do something with it. There were always offers from "Less Wild Lovers" (as my friends John and Brent call addictions). The refrigerator was always available. Disconnected chitchat was always there on Facebook. On-line relationships and trysts that offered relief for a weekend here and there were available. There's an endless list; you fill in the blank. I tried a few, of course, but always found that they were not big enough to hold my heart.

I had to keep my heart open to my very specific desire—to be married to a strong, good-hearted man who wanted to honor God with his life. I needed to hold that ache *while* I took long hikes, *while* I made a lingering meal for friends, *while* I explored how to be involved in issues of exploitation without a partner to share it with. I had to find God's embrace for my open, aching heart in the meantime—*while I waited*. I am convinced it is from that place—*the meantime*—that all true beauty flows. When we resist openhearted dreaming, the bitch rushes in to praise us for being smart enough not to dream. When we live from openhearted desire, the bitch is there, mocking us as fools.

Staying Alive Midst Our Pain

The bitch was lurking in the shadows as Steve and I opened ourselves to another level of dreaming: the dream of a child. I'm grateful to say she did not win, but beauty in the midst of such tender, tender dreaming is hard won. As we've said, beauty always rises, but sometimes she rises while shielding her eyes and trembling.

You see, Steve and I experienced a miracle. Even my doctor did not deny it. Several doctors told us it would be impossible for us to conceive a child, our own child, a child bearing our bloodline and genetics.

We asked so many doctors, hoping for one to give us a shred of possibility. But after a string of disappointing conversations, we came to terms with the fact that the cocktail of quirky genes from our colorful families would likely not emerge into the world as a curly-haired bundle of energy toddling across our lawn.

I was older when we married, so our desire to have our own child had the potential to be simply foolish. But there had been a sense of promise which we did not seek. Maybe it was divine prophecy. Maybe it was what psychologists call *magical thinking*, an imagination born of sheer desire. All we knew is that it trekked us like a puppy pulling on the hem of our jeans. Delightful, but irritating. By the time we spoke with the fourth doctor, the promise felt cruel.

Then, suddenly: the miracle. The unexpected word "pregnant" appeared. My concrete-thinking, process-guy husband broke into a giddy dance. We twirled like children at the thought of spending the upcoming spring celebrating the resurrection of life. We would eventually come up to Holy Week in anticipation of a child. I went into shock. As the time unfolded, all was heightened. The fledgling grass was pungent as I knelt to pull dead growth from the rose garden. I flooded quietly with wonder, a sensuality I had never known—not quite, anyway. A sense of completeness descended. I rehearsed the moments when we would tell my best friend, my sister. I ached for missing my mom.

And then, as powerfully as life came, it quietly left in a mass of tissue, tears, and bewilderment. The miracle disappeared in the early morning hours of Palm Sunday.

We were so, so sad.

We huddled in our down-filled bed and stared at each other, too sad to cry.

What is the heart to do with a God who arouses, stirs up longing up from the dust of dead dreams, only to have them catch the slightest curl up into the breeze. God's breath wafted over the empty canvas of my womb, breathing in newness of life, but then it seemed he breathed out, leaving a space into which my heart would free-fall. We had experienced God as more powerful than the nature itself. Then we found him maddening. Steve unabashedly proclaimed out loud to his God that morning, "Don't mess with me." With these words he worshipped, in defense of his wounded heart, or, as our friend Dan says, "Good hearts are captured in a divine wrestling match; fearful, doubting hearts stay clear of the mat."[22] Steve went to the mat that morning, in a glorious way only God knows.

As I mentioned, it was Palm Sunday. Steve finally forced himself out of bed in a kind attempt to bring comfort to me by going to the grocery store for some breakfast items. He came home bearing a bouquet of flowers. They were beautiful—white lilies, chrysanthemums, roses, and two simple palm branches. Someone had fun with that, Steve mused. We imagined someone in the grocery store floral department, choosing the palm branches in private solidarity with the faith they held dear, in a culture for which palm branches hold little meaning against the backdrop of Cadbury eggs and sugared chicks.

We pulled the palm branches out and went back to bed, waving them as we went, in a slightly embarrassed passion play of our own, reenacting a feeble triumphal entry of Jesus into our bed of sorrow, our place of mourning, our sackcloth and ashes.

We decided to read the familiar Palm Sunday passage of scripture. What else were we to do? If you've ever grieved, you know that sometimes you just have to do the normal thing, the ritual thing, because you just don't know what else *to* do.

So we read.

The cast of characters tumbled out into our foggy grief with surprising comfort. Here was Martha working hard on a feast for Jesus, still in shock from seeing Lazarus alive. Here was Mary, true to her grateful self, offering a lovely but seductive gesture when she allows her hair to fall on Jesus' feet as she splashes them with perfume. Here was Judas self-righteously complaining.

Somewhere in the story, Jesus says, "You will not always have Me." He was preparing to say yes to his own death, his own crushing of hope, his own dark struggle unto resurrected fulfillment. He was also preparing his friends to live in the free-falling bewilderment of being *without* him.

Through His words, Jesus was preparing his followers to live in the vacuum, the fright that comes when we just can't see him, the scary nature of the *meantime*. I am his follower. His encouragement came several hours too late, but the words held me up, somehow.

We will not always have him. That is terrifying. He warns us, prepares us for this, telling us that he leaves us sometimes. That is kind. But between haunting promise and triumph, between the coronation of dreams and unmet dreams, we trek through the corridor of death, betrayal, and abandonment.

We are, gratefully, given the promise of a Comforter. And the Spirit is real. It's just that our pain blocks our hearing; we can't always hear the Spirit with perfect clarity. So we have to trust his heart when he says he'll come back.

You might be familiar with the scene from *The Last of the Mohicans* when Nathaniel Hawkeye (Daniel Day Lewis—sigh) arrives with Cora (Madeline Stowe) behind a waterfall after being pursued by Magua (Wes Studi), a Huron chief who has sworn to wipe out her family line. When Hawkeye realizes that he must carry on without her in order to continue the fight, he prepares her for the fact that he is about to leave her to be captured by Magua. He must leave her in enemy hands. He passionately insists, "You stay alive. If they don't kill you, they'll take you north up to Huron lands. You submit, do you hear? You're strong. You survive. You stay alive no matter what occurs. I will find you…no matter how long it takes, no matter how far. I will find you."

This scene really does capture why it is so difficult to not deaden ourselves—whether through addiction to Glenlivet or through a more daily resignation into sub-humanness through something like much of talk radio. Why in the world would we want to stay alive when the one who is supposed to love us and protect us has just handed us over into enemy hands? That's how it feels, anyway. This is why it is easier on a long afternoon to just let our thoughts glaze over, dreaming of a doughnut or sneaking a shot or mulling over a choice piece of gossip, rather than envisioning ways we can tell an elderly relative a joke, tend to our tomato plants, help a child draw, or work on a novel. Beauty stirs us awake. Addiction warns us to stay dull. During those moments, we forget the Larger Story; we forget that the one who *seems to* have vanished is actually out fighting a greater war on our behalf. "In a little while," says Jesus. "In a little while I will return for you." Oh, that "little while" is rough, to say the least. We are taken by Magua to Huron land and beyond. Staying alive feels impossible, yet it is what we are asked to do.

In our bed that Palm Sunday, I felt so sad that Jesus had left me—that is, that he had left me with this unrequited desire. But somehow I was also incredibly comforted that he *told me* that he would leave me sometimes. This held me as I crumpled with the comforter around my neck. I didn't have him,

then. But I know him. I've *learned* him; studied him
as one studies the ways of their lover. And I knew he
would come back for my heart, sometime, when I was
ready. I did not recognize it, but resurrection was
already on its way. It took me months to live in to this
reality, but it was true.

That kind of Larger Story reassurance is the only
thing that assuages the bitch—she is in the background,
chanting, "You fool, you dreaming fool." Beauty says, "It
is okay to surrender. I'm remembered in this seemingly
cruel meantime." Beauty waits for life to return when all
life seems lost.

So what we are saying is this: you have no
guarantees, but dream anyway. You will hurt more if
it doesn't work out, but your laugh will have a more
rapt quality to it. You'll feel the sting, but your face
will glisten with the fresh dew of presence. You will
love more, you will feel the air in your lungs, you will
feel boulders of sadness on your heart, but you'll be
alive. And you'll be okay. Saint Bartholomew said,
"Many of us spend our whole lives running from
feeling with the mistaken belief that you cannot bear
the pain. But you have already borne the pain; what
you have not done is feel all you are beyond the pain."
Exactly. Jesus did not say, "I will rescue you out of
your disappointing world." He did say, "The thief
comes to steal and destroy, but I have come that you
would have life and have it abundantly" (John 10:10).

I can hear the bitch coming to the fragile part of
you, which has been so disappointed, saying, "So
we're supposed to believe that there is abundant life

in miscarriages?" The bitch gathers all the data she can find to prove that God has abandoned you and is callous, so you might as well shut down through any number of means. It seems reasonable, after all, to eat copious amounts of ice cream in a dissociative fugue after a bewildering miscarriage. Doesn't it? Well, maybe for a little while. Ice cream actually works really well for me—for a time. But those jaunts into oblivion are just not strong enough to comfort.

The abundant life comes when we allow our wounded hearts to be uncovered so that it can be bandaged, cared for, and healed. Only when we remove the earplugs of our denial can we hear the reassuring voice of the one who appears to have left, but wants to comfort—and will come again. "I will never leave you nor forsake you" takes on a whole new intimacy. Dallas Willard says it well: "It is being included in the . . . life of God that heals all wounds and allows us to stop demanding satisfaction. What really matters -once it is clear that you are included? You have been chosen. God chooses you. This is the message of the kingdom."[23] This is the news your heart has always wanted to hear. And if you'll quiet her skepticism, this news just may settle the bitch down, bringing her the comfort she needs. As the Apostle Peter says, "You love him even though you have never seen him. Though you do not see him now, you trust him; and you rejoice with a glorious, inexpressible joy" (I Peter 1:8).

My favorite passage of scripture is Romans 8:35-37. It is a stabilizing message—an invitation to stay present in the midst of things that rend our hearts. Paul, who has suffered unthinkable trauma in his life with God, provides the final arbiter of whether or not we are justified in shutting down, dissociating or fleeing into addiction:

> Can anything ever separate us from Christ's love? Does it mean he no longer loves us if we have trouble or calamity, or are persecuted, or hungry, or destitute, or in danger, or threatened with death? (As the Scriptures say, "For your sake we are killed every day; we are being slaughtered like sheep.") No, despite all these things, overwhelming victory is ours through Christ, who loved us.

> And I am convinced that nothing can ever separate us from God's love. Neither death nor life, neither angels nor demons, neither our fears for today nor our worries about tomorrow—not even the powers of hell can separate us from God's love. No power in the sky above or in the earth below—indeed, nothing in all creation will ever be able to separate us from the love of God that is revealed in Christ Jesus our Lord.

We are not promised that we will be spared the calamity of learning disabilities, persecution of our substance, danger or threat against our sexuality, demonic attack or even the powers of hell. But we are promised—and this promise is everything—that none of those things can keep us from being loved, and knowing we are loved, and loving in return. This gives me strength to live as Mary Oliver says in her poem "When Death Comes": "I don't want to end up simply having visited this world." No, we get to unpack and move in—show up—and make this sad place beautiful again.

Why would we spend our energy trying to separate from God, from ourselves, and from the world, when Jesus has pulled out all the stops so that we wouldn't be separated from him? Rhetorical question, of course. But why would we?

The Last-Minute God

I wish for a different God. I really do. I wish I had a God who would take his paintbrush and paint peace on every hurting face I have ever seen. I want him to paint fulfillment into the demeanor of a vivacious, gorgeous, athletic friend who, in her single thirties, aches for a family of her own. On the faces of scores of kids I know in Sri Lanka, now teenagers trying to make it without parents because a goliath wave came and wiped out their world, along with a quarter of a million people, in a half an hour. I wish God would paint restoration into the body of a friend who, after she uprooted, trained, and transferred cultures in order to serve exploited women in Cambodia, got raped herself by a policeman. Or in the eyes of the client whose father put a noose around my client's neck and made him stand on a bucket, taunting him with false kicks toward the bucket, just to see him squirm.

But that's just it—we don't imagine that God can use his brush in that staggering, healing way, smack dab in the middle of such pain. We don't imagine that he wants to or believe that he will, because we have listened to the taunts of skeptical resignation. But he can. I've seen it. God can come, bind up the broken-hearted, and set the captive free. It is just that the captivity from which we are freed is often more of the self-imposed kind—prisons of bitterness that fuel revenge-filled bouts with sexual promiscuity, doubt about God's goodness which seems to justify overeating, and flights into fantasy that has almost destroyed many friends' marriage and has succeeded in others. It is the mission of Jesus to come to us *there*. The addicted bitch in us is too busy being lazy to dream that it could be true: Jesus wants to bring healing, even in the midst of the pain, especially the pain of disappointed longings.

As my friend Stasi says, "Our God is a God of last-minute deliverances." That's an understatement. And after a miscarriage, or a rape, or a childhood of abuse, the last minute seems to have evaporated, and he is simply too late. The Lord said to his prophet, Jeremiah, "They will fight against you but will not overcome you, for I am with you and will rescue you," (Jeremiah 1:19). Stasi muses, " Ummmm . . . when did God rescue him exactly? After he was beaten. After he was imprisoned. After he was threatened, opposed, and thrown into a cistern. Yes, God's view is dramatically different from ours. Jeremiah went through much travail. So has every saint before him and after him, though not all to that extreme. And regardless of what comes our way, God tells all of us, "Don't be afraid." He says, "My grace is sufficient for you."[24]

We are not delivered from our circumstances, though that is what we demand. No, we are delivered from the ways we attempt to create a world where our circumstances are not real. As our friend Larry imagines God saying, "I rescued Jeremiah—and I will rescue you—from faithless unbelief, from hopeless despair, and from unloving self-obsession."[25] Then He gives us a reality beyond our wildest dreams. He meets us in that deepest longing.

I know a man whose family can be rightly called evil. The coldness of the way his family gave him over to be sexually abused by his aunt is too much to tell on these pages. His deepest wound as a young boy was being taught that he had no strength; that he was only there for the servicing of women. It is impossible to tell you the story of how Jesus came for his heart—beauty is like that, remember? But Jesus knew exactly how to do it. This man had to address many addictive patterns in his life—predictably, addictions fueled by shame and degradation. But Jesus knew what his deeper longing was, deeper than freedom in the realm of sex, deeper than a vibrant marriage.

He, his wife, and I were in conversation one day about himself as a boy, caught in that powerless trap. We decided to pray. I heard Jesus say that there was something about a tree. I said (saying as you do when you know you must speak but are feeling sheepish and cautious), "Uh, Jesus says there is something about a tree." This friend stopped for a long moment to consider, then was undone in tears. He explained that Jesus reminded him of a memory he had long forgotten: that when he was eight he went out from his aunt's house in the middle of the night, with an ax bigger than his little frame, and he began chopping his aunt's favorite tree down. He chopped and chopped until his little hands were bleeding, until his abuser's tree fell down. You can imagine the healing, the confirmation of his strength, that came from that encounter.

Jesus is like that. Not always that obvious, but always that intentional.

Stay alive, dear addicted sister. You are not the detached bitch you thought you were, and you don't have to become one. Walk away from the fourth cookie. Flee the conversations with the unavailable man. Bless your feminine body that has suffered rather than making it suffer more. There is comfort for you—there really is. And you have beauty to bring this world that is all your own. You have suspected it, and it is true: beauty can be found *anywhere*. And beauty can be *brought* anywhere.

The love of God is either real or it is not, and I'm telling you: it is real. Stay present. It is worth the cost.

---

[14] Jan Meyers, *The Allure of Hope* (Colorado Springs: Navpress, 2000), 84.

[15] Madeleine L'Engle, *Walking on Water: Reflections on Art and Faith* (Colorado Springs: Shaw, 2001), 114, 234.

[16] Dan Allender, *The Wounded Heart* (Colorado Springs: Navpress, 1990), p. 199

[17] Winn Collier, "Tell Me the Truth", from Church at deeperstory.com, February, 2013.

[18] C.S. Lewis, *The Weight of Glory* (San Francisco: HarperCollins, 1949), p.29.

[19] World Youth Day, Rome, August 19, 2000.

[20] Sharon Hersh, *The Last Addiction* (Colorado Springs: Waterbrook, 2008), 183.

[21] Gerald May, *Addiction and Grace: Love and Spirituality in the Healing of Addictions* (San Francisco: Harper, 1988), 94.

[22] Allender, *The Wounded Heart*, 192.

[23] Dallas Willard, *The Divine Conspiracy* (New York, NY: Harper Collins, 1998), 340.

[24] Stasi Eldredge, *Becoming Myself* (Colorado Springs: David C. Cook, 2013),91.

[25] Larry Crabb, *God's Love Letters to You* (Nashville: Thomas Nelson, 2010), 44.

Chapter Five

Restoration: How Beauty Trumps Bitch

Quit believing the lie that your worst mistake defines who you are

> ~ Bob Goff

Grace was in her steps, heaven in her eye, in every gesture dignity and love.

> ~ John Milton

They will sparkle in his land like jewels in a crown. How wonderful and beautiful they will be!

> ~ Zechariah

Your heart is safe.

Wouldn't it be great if you believed that? Wouldn't it be amazing if the bitch inside of you *wasn't needed* anymore? If she became convinced that you are safe, maybe she could, I don't know, take an early retirement on Kauai or something. If your heart was quieted, and the bitch was comforted by the fact that you are okay, that she doesn't need to protect you anymore . . . wow, just think.

You can be as loving as you want to be. You can express your gratitude generously. Your kindness can surface, in simple and extravagant ways. Your face can lose its shadow. You can look people in the eye, not look down. You can be yourself and not some fabricated version of you. Your passionate heart can beat like an African djembe when it needs to be; you can be calm as Sonora when you want to be. You can feel gorgeous in your own skin. You will want to "clothe yourself with the beauty that comes from within, the unfading beauty of a gentle and quiet spirit, which is so precious to God"[5] because you won't feel the need to prove anything. You can go crazy with fashion if you desire, but you won't fret about it. You know your substance is only made more beautiful when your spirit is like a calm ocean— powerful, but not foaming or churning.

All of the above, because you have learned that the only one big enough to protect your heart is Jesus Christ. He doesn't promise blanket protection for your life; on the contrary, he warns of just how dangerous following him can be. You've probably heard Mrs. Beaver's laugh when she thinks of Aslan: "Oh, he's good, but he's not safe. He's the king, I tell you!" I have a sentence in my bio that says that he has messed up my well-planned life. He's not a safe God, but your heart is safe *in* him. He is committed to finding, loving, disarming, comforting and freeing your heart, and releasing its beauty.

And since the bitch is leaving her post, it is okay to soften, to open, and to receive. Really, it's okay. It is okay to relax, to exhale, to have that glass of wine if alcohol is good to you; it's okay to allow your husband's gaze. It is okay to be stirred by a kind touch, a kiss of warm wind on a summer's evening, the giggle of a toddler, or the swell of a tide of worship, or a really good romp in the hay with your spouse.

It is possible. Love can trump your fear, and the hilarity of God can trump your pride. Your shame can be trumped by his mercy and your rage by his kindness. The exhausting demands of your addiction can be crowded out and silenced by one thing: the undeserved grace of God and his pursuit of your heart despite your dark side. Grace sees the ugly and says, "I'm going to release the beauty anyway." Your beauty will win as you are caught off guard by Jesus, who celebrates you even though you don't trust him.

Hopefully it is clear by now—we mar beauty in many ways, through all the ways mentioned, and at least, oh, hundreds more. But hopefully it is even *clearer* that our beauty cannot be destroyed even through our worst moments. As a line from a song by the group *Noah and the Whale* says, "My love surrounds you like an ether in everything you do." The Apostle Paul said the same thing in a slightly more theological tone: "For God was in Christ, reconciling the world to himself, no longer counting people's sins against them" (2 Cor. 5:9)

The Gift of Dignity

There is no penalty for your bad behavior. Of course you feel the consequences of your dark side (your relationship has taken a hit because of control, your pride has isolated you, your addiction has affected your health), but there is no changing the fact that God is crazy about you. He bestowed the beauty, and what he makes can't be destroyed. What dignity this provides us! The Apostle Paul says, "For we are God's masterpiece. He has created us anew in Christ Jesus, so we can do the good things he planned for us long ago" (Eph. 2:10). The Greek the word for masterpiece is *poema*, which is where we get our English word poem. You are the poem of God. You are his piece of art. And artists do not like their masterpieces to be messed with. Artists know that the core meaning and value of their creation can never be eradicated, even if one tries to pervert it, misinterpret it, or destroy it. This Artist knows what he meant to say when he created you—his knowledge of your deepest heart is what gives you dignity.

Jesus was fighting for our dignity when he gave the Sermon on the Mount. It is not a sermon about correct Christian doctrine as much as Jesus giving us a new way to see ourselves, our relationships, and especially our core need of his grace. And it is a sermon tailor-made for us if we have hearts that grieve the trail of damage our dark side leaves behind. We find in this sermon the beatitudes, which just might be the most splendid vision for beautiful living ever cast. And then Jesus begins to move in to the crowd. If you listen closely to Jesus' engagement with the people listening that day, you can imagine a glint in his eye—it is almost as if he was winking at those in the crowd who were actually there to learn from his heart. Don't imagine a flippant wink—no, imagine the wink a Father gives his child when the child is in the process of seeing something for the first time. And yet in the same breath he was indicting the

Pharisees who were listening for the sheer purpose of catching him teaching some aberration of the religious law. "You have heard it said," Jesus says, "But I say to you..." *Depend on my way of seeing,* he says. *You don't see clearly.* This way of seeing—the clarity-producing lens which Jesus puts on our eyes—leads to freedom. This sermon with its shrewd wisdom exposes all that is not free or saturated in grace.

Jesus is the plumb line of justice, and he, in this one event, renders all of us silent and without excuse. Jesus cocks his head in bemusement at all the ways we try to justify, keep score, grade ourselves for our righteousness. He winks as he exposes how silly it all is that we would think we would not wander nor fail him. In the Sermon on the Mount, Jesus creates a level playing field where a woman realizes that her lustful demand for an Audi A6 is equal to the obvious shame of the "brazen adulteress" who was found sleeping with her son's teacher; where a woman whose catty gossip has destroyed someone's reputation realizes what she has in common with a death row murderer; where a woman who worked diligently to recruit others to her religious organization realizes she has no audience with Jesus to display years of what she thought were impressive displays of her devotion. He cocks his head and slyly says, "I have always been clear that I look to the heart. Why would you think it would be any different?" What dignity this gives to those who understand their frailty, those who are not shocked by their propensity toward adultery of heart and murder in thought, those who simply long to fall at Jesus' feet with matted hair, in gratitude that he sees them and adores them still.

As we keep listening to Jesus' sermon, our hearts grow a bit lighter.

His teaching on divorce at first seems quite harsh, but wait: he seems to be indicating that, although tragic, *of course* there will be divorce as long as there are hard hearts in the world. And he's already pushed the boundary lines of adultery to include, well, everyone, so there's that level playing field again. His teaching on the need to be as holy as the Pharisees sounds impossible, but wait: he seems to have a grin on his face when he says it. "As if you would get there on your own," he seems to say. As my friend John says, Jesus is saying, "Oh, you *will* be holy . . ." but Jesus is making it clear to everyone in the crowd that it is not possible without his life inside of us. The condition of our hearts is too grave. Jesus knows that the only hope is his grace extended to adulterous, murderous hearts, and the full restoration that comes from his death, burial, and resurrection.

And then, to cover all the bases, Jesus provides the courage to offer your right cheek to someone who has humiliated you by slapping you to the ground. In the ancient Near East, a person suffered total degradation when slapped by someone's left hand, the hand that no Hebrew would use to touch another because it was the hand for wiping at the toilet. To be slapped in this way was a statement that you had no value whatsoever. It is what we have come to know as treating someone like a piece of shit. Jesus knew that in order to offer the right cheek, you'd have to get up off the floor and stand up with dignity in the presence of your degrading tormenter—you'd have to stand in order to offer the cheek. Jesus knew that the posture required to turn the other cheek is one of dignity, one that says, "You have taken what you have taken, but you cannot have my dignity or my heart. If you really want to try, go ahead. You have been destructive, but my dignity is indestructible."

By the end of the sermon, there is not one in the crowd who has not been dignified by the only one with the true authority to bestow such honor.

An Indian friend of mine, from Kolkata, lives the power of turning the other cheek, and she knows the kind of creative, extravagant giving that can flow from it. Years ago, through the encouragement of a friend, she sought counseling and began a process of healing from sexual abuse from an uncle. She told the story for the first time—named it as abusive and damaging, and she began, tentatively, to admit how powerless she felt to stop the abuse because of her uncle's threats. She felt her dignity returning as she named how evil had tried to destroy her beauty.

Around the time this healing was occurring, this woman heard a guest lecturer reveal the staggering number of Nepali girls who were being trapped in slavery in Mumbai after being drugged and taken into India across the Nepal border. She felt an immediate affinity for these girls, which caught her by surprise. She was overwhelmed with the thought of the futility of these girls' lives. Something about their lack of control, their inability to change things, haunted her.

This woman determined to do something bordering on ludicrous. "I just didn't know what else to do," she said, as most of us would in the face of the unmanageable problem. She and her girlfriend traveled to Mumbai and entered one of the bars that had a reputation as a front for prostitution. As their eyes adjusted to the dark entryway, they saw six young teenage girls, in the regalia of seduction, painted and frosted and shining from gloss. The girls' eyes were hollow, straining to engage the customers as they paraded and curved their limbs and bodies around the poles on the platform. Without thinking too clearly, this courageous, crazy friend of mine jumped up on the platform, fully clothed, diverting the eyes of the patrons from the working girls. The customers went silent from shock for a fraction of a second, but the silence quickly gave way to rage. They began pulling at my friend's jeans and demanding that she stop interrupting the show. As the steaming mad manager descended from the loft, my friend climbed down and looked up at the sixteen year old next to her on the platform (whose mouth was gaping over what she had just witnessed). My friend whispered to her, "I know what I just did is crazy, but I wanted you to know what it was like to not have consuming eyes on you for just a moment or two. You are worth more than that."

Shine More

Now, I'm going to say something here that may seem to completely contradict the fact that your heart is safe with God, but we have to explore this if we're going to feel released to be glorious, without self-protecting. There's a flip side to cultivating our beauty, and that is this: beauty is rarely welcomed. We hear this alluded to in more of Pope John Paul II's words about Jesus: "It is He who reads in your heart your most genuine choices, the choices that others try to stifle."

I've been getting to know a woman I previously knew only by reputation. She is a lovely and witty person, and also has a weighty, intelligent presence, the kind that calls everyone in the room to attention. She has a winsome spirit and a deep soul. She is genuinely kind. And her physical beauty will knock you over—bright green eyes, shimmering hair, creamy complexion, and a fantastic physique.

We pine to be her, right? Well, yes, but we have to remember that beauty provokes. What I mean is, you can't stay neutral in the presence of beauty like this woman's. Beauty requires a response from those who see it and encounter it. And as you probably know from your own life, beauty is not always welcomed. Sometimes it is harmed. Sometimes it is ignored. Sometimes it is consumed.

Sometimes it is our substance that becomes the target of envy. Sometimes it is the physical that provokes lust, like that of the lovely Caroline in the movie *Enchanted April*, who said, "I've wasted so much time being beautiful." Caroline was weary of being pawed at, not for her substance, but for her sexuality. Beauty threatens because it exposes the lack in those around it. When I am around luminous skin, I become aware of my freckles and wrinkles. When I am around a vibrant spirit, I feel the sagging quality of my weary soul. Released and true beauty invites envy, and therefore it invites attack.

This beautiful woman tells me of her experience in a graduate degree program at an established, reputable seminary, where she was working toward a Master's degree in Theology. You would think that in pursuit of such a degree that her efforts would be encouraged, that she would be appreciated for her intellect as well as her presence. But it is there that she has had vicious lies spread about her, instructors tear down her contributions in class, and an overall experience of ostracism. Now, we might expect a certain good ol' boys club at a seminary, but the truth is that there were many female students in the same degree program, and others were doing well, left alone, their efforts lauded. These experiences had her swirling in confusion, and she was beginning to ingest their accusations and opinions of her. She was starting to get insecure.

One day a professor called this woman into his office. He told her he had noticed the treatment she was receiving, and he said, "I have only one thing to say to you." Pause. "*Shine more.*"

She was stunned. It was as if his words washed over her like a cleansing bath. She felt so understood and believed in. This professor recognized that she was being hated for carrying the life of God inside her, for displaying his image in an unmuted, un-neutered, shimmering display. She was being despised for the beauty she brings, and this professor was wise enough and kind enough to recognize it.

Beauty threatens, beauty is hated, and beauty is attacked. The prophet Ezekiel describes the king of Tyre, who was a tyrannical, wicked man—think Ahmadinejad, Bashar al-Assad, or Mugabe. Many scholars believe that the description of him is in fact a description of evil itself, Satan's essence and personality. As you read this description, listen to how stunning something that is now evil was *before* it was corrupted:

> You were the model of perfection, full of wisdom and exquisite in beauty. You were in Eden, the garden of God. Your clothing was adorned with every precious stone—red carnelian, pale-green peridot, white moonstone, blue-green beryl, onyx, green jasper, blue lapis lazuli, turquoise, and emerald—all beautifully crafted for you and set in the finest gold (Ez. 28:11-13).

We don't usually think of evil as sensual, brilliant, luminous; but in its original state, it would have slayed us with its beauty. Listen to the position given to this majestic being, and the beginning of the corruption:

> I ordained and anointed you as the mighty angelic guardian. You had access to the holy mountain of God and walked among the stones of fire. You were blameless in all you did from the day you were created until the day evil was found in you. Your rich commerce led you to violence, and you sinned. So I banished you in disgrace from the mountain of God. I expelled you, O mighty guardian, from your place among the stones of fire (14)

Then the phrase that captures what seduced Lucifer, taking him down:

> Your heart was filled with pride
> because of all your beauty.
> Your wisdom was corrupted
> by your love of splendor (17).

Evil was banished from the presence of God because it wanted beauty all for itself; it wanted to be the glory, to have the glory, and not to reflect glory. It wanted possession. And it is clear, as we look back over season and epochs of time on this earth, that ever since it was banished, evil has had a furious, envious, lustful desire to destroy anything that is beautiful—especially the beauty of Jesus in you.

The description does not make sense without the context of the Larger Story of the scriptures, and as my friends John and Brent point out, the story does not begin in the garden of Eden. It begins in a war in heaven, as Lucifer, the gloriously beautiful angel, becomes determined to have for himself all the affection of the Father's heart that was lavished on Jesus. Lucifer could not stand to play second fiddle, let alone remain in a position of "longing to understand God's heart." We all know the rest of the story: cast out, bringing legions of fallen angels with him, evil is now intent on destroying what it could not possess freely, what it lost. The image of God, the life of Christ, the beauty you carry—these are now the targets. And sadly, we are often the ones who join in when we judge, are threatened by, and tear down another's beauty, whether in hidden thoughts or overt attitudes.

It takes more maturity to revel in another woman's beauty at a dinner party than it does to teach an entire seminar on being a Christian woman.

Shine in Your Uniqueness

Perhaps as you are reading this you are thinking, "I can appreciate others' glory, but being a target? No, this doesn't really apply to me because my beauty isn't strong enough to provoke anything." Think again—please think again. Sometimes it is the very impediments we assume are ugly that are surprisingly seen by others as beautiful. We can apply the words from the epistle: "His power is made perfect in weakness." Where you think you are weak in beauty, maybe, just maybe someone else delights in—or is threatened by—that very thing.

Imagine Fred Astaire and Ginger Rogers. Ah, their floating, elegant, masterful way on the dance floor. They make it look easy; their finesse is all that shows even though their bodies are taxed from the sheer athleticism of their craft. I enjoy thinking about them. They make me happy. And they make me yearn to be elegant on the dance floor.

Then look at a picture of two buildings along a riverfront in Prague that serve as the National Building for the Czech Republic. The colloquial name for these odd buildings is Fred and Ginger. They are humorously called the *Tančící dům*, or The Dancing House, because they look like partners, barely holding each other up. Designed in the 1990's by American architect Frank Gehry and Czech architect Vlad Milunic, the buildings look almost disheveled, but they have been lauded as exquisite. I promise you—these buildings themselves are not what we might normally consider beautiful. They clash with the gothic architecture in this gorgeous city of spires. But Former Czech President Vaclav Havel, who lives close by, loves them.[26] They are a refreshing presence, a lyrical relief from the heavy history the other buildings in Prague hold within their walls.

Don't underestimate the power of your uniqueness.

Shine as the Kingdom Comes to You on Earth

Sometimes the thing that makes us shine comes when we encounter the Kingdom of heaven as it breaks through into our lives on earth. The Celtic Christians called those encounters liminal spaces, when the veil between *here* and *there* is very slight. And these encounters—like all beauty—require a response.

I had one of those encounters when Steve and I went to the enchanted little mountain town of Crested Butte in Central Colorado, just as the aspen were beginning to crest, when you can feel the heat slowly seeping from the earth, yawning and beginning its slow turn into sleep. It was perfect. We needed this little getaway, and the atmosphere ushered us quickly into a lazy state of being.

We spent two days hiking into the Maroon Bells Wilderness. We didn't attack the trail, but instead we took our time, drinking in pine, spruce, gold and crimson aspen, and the smell of wet riverbeds. And we enjoyed an unusually high volume of raptors in the air—eagles, hawks, a falcon, some osprey. Raptor sightings have always brought us strength. As we walked, Steve admitted to me, with vulnerable shyness, "I would really love to, finally, see an owl." Steve knew I have had a few sacred encounters with owls, and I knew it took a lot of courage for him to admit his longing for this—again. You see, Steve had been praying for two years to see an owl. We hear them occasionally near our home, but his eyes have never, in all his Colorado years, feasted on one. The desire runs deep and he, like all of us, wonders if God cares about those desires.

I love owls, everything about them. I love their puffy baby feathers when they are little, I love the way their eyes know things, things from other worlds. I love their wingspans, their stealth flight patterns, their ethereal calls in the night. As we continued on the trail, I quietly whispered my request, "Jesus, it would be great if you would bring an owl to delight Steve's heart." We returned to the little European-style lodge where we were staying, having seen no owl, but our surroundings were too lovely for us to be too disappoint

On our last night, Steve wanted to do some reading, and I felt the Spirit nudging me outside one last time: *Come look at the stars.* I knew that to get the best view possible of the celestial blanket that hangs low in the mountains, I needed to get away from town. So I drove as the sun was setting. And I drove, and the sun kept setting. And I drove. I found a serpentine side road that began to climb. Hairpin turn, climb, hairpin turn up, up past some secluded private roads. The sky was beginning to deepen, but I only saw one star. So I kept driving.

After almost twenty minutes of low-grade light, the road ended. At this point I was on a ridge high above Crested Butte, so I decided to get out and walk around a bit. The trees were dense and I couldn't really see over the edge, so I began to walk into the woods, toward what looked like a clearing. Finally, the forest was darkening, so I hoped to find a spot and—finally—watch the stars come out.

Suddenly, I felt a rush of air over my head and saw the slightest shadow. From the corner of my eye I saw a large bird, moving through the trees. I wondered if it was a raptor. I smiled to think of it flying near me.

Then I felt it again, this time right—as in *directly*—over my head. I could discern that its body had some bulk, so I felt confident that it was a raptor. But again it had disappeared. Suddenly—*whoosh*. No, wait—*whoosh*. Oh my goodness, that was two of them! I ducked just a bit, hearing nothing, but watching the forms of two flying creatures come to rest on the branch of a sparse ponderosa pine. After they lit on the branch, I could see their outline.

Owls. Those are owls! I was thrilled. As I studied the two, again I felt it: *whoosh, whoosh*. I felt two more, but this time I saw stocky little creatures—round-shouldered, stubby little wings, which also landed, and looked like little Yodas in the tree. I realized that these were very young owls, and they began calling to each other from tree to tree with a high, quick screech—the cry of adolescence.

The low, circular flight over my head continued. Owls circled, watching me, checking me out. One after the other after the other. I would watch two land, and three more would descend. I counted eleven all together. At one point I dropped to my knees in the pine needles, partly to take a bit of cover under my own arms, and partly because that's what happens in the midst of glory. I could not decide whether to laugh or cry. So I did both. There were no

witnesses, just me and the little army of old and
young wise creatures, swarming like bees. Jesus just
kept asking the same question: "Do you like it?" My
answer came out as a delighted belly laugh of a *yes*.

And now it was dark. I backed out of the woods
slowly, sad that it had to end.

When I got to the car, after shaking off a bit of the
adrenaline, a terrible thought hit me: Steve.

I wanted to race down the hill, barge into the
room and share it with him. But I felt tentative,
careful with his heart. I didn't want to step on his
desires, tread on that tender place in all of us which
quietly wonders, "Why not me, God?" But I also
knew I wanted to respect Steve enough to handle the
disappointment in order to rejoice with me. I thought
about all the times I have told female clients to allow
their men to have broad shoulders for them. My turn.

I decided to risk it. It would be disappointing to
him, I knew. I also knew that he loves it when my heart
is delighted, and he would be thrilled on my behalf. I
drove back and opened the door to the room, albeit
tentatively. He immediately saw the glory in my eyes
(I wouldn't have been able to hide it anyway). I sat
down on the bed, quiet for a few moments, then told
him. A moment's disappointment crested in his eyes,
and then a surge of excitement for me came. He was
genuinely in awe. We shared the magic of it for a while,
and then I was able to care for him, inquiring about his
heart in light of his prayers.

That is a delicate dance, isn't it? If I had rushed
into the room, hiding the glory I had just basked in,

trying to protect his heart without letting him be strong for me first, I'm pretty sure he would have felt it as mothering. As it was, I could bask in his joy, we could laugh and stand in wonder together, and *then* I could turn with care for the tender heart of a strong man, the man I had just allowed to be strong. So instead of a mother, I could be Steve's lover.

If you prayed the Lord's Prayer that day, I appreciate it, because the kingdom came to me on earth as it is in heaven. The beauty of that kingdom invites us to be kind and it calls us to be respectful. Kingdom beauty hesitates; it doesn't move or speak abruptly. It considers. But the beauty of heaven, when it shows up on earth, also compels us to take risks. Beauty rarely, if ever, descends on us so we can play it safe through hiding or control.

As my friend Dan says, "The heavens and earth will one day be so free of blight, heartache, and sin that the creation will come to play with the kings and queens of creation: you and me." Well, a glimpse of that day descended on me, and it was a blast.

Those on-earth-as-it-is-in-heaven moments tickle us, elbow us with a sense of what is coming. They give us a taste the sheer magic of that place. It wasn't just the owls that were the taste of heaven (though I swear I saw them slip through the veil). No, it was what happened *in* me. Frederic Buechner says, "There is a kind of high comedy about seeing and not seeing, about waiting, about being human but not quite human." There was something about that mystical mountain moment *here* that made me more of the human I will be *there*.

And there's no question that brilliant comedy was at play. The best comedy takes a portion of what is real and magnifies it, right? Well, all I can tell you is, because of that encounter, I am positive that the coming kingdom will be saturated with baffling encounters with the Creation. As Buechner goes on to say, "You hardly know whether to laugh or to weep. Well, laugh then, since you have to choose one or the other."[27] No, we don't know whether to laugh or cry when we get hints and glimmers of what is coming. Peter says that even the prophets "wondered what time or situation the Spirit of Christ within them was talking about when he told them in advance about Christ's suffering and his great glory afterward . . . . It is all so wonderful that even the angels are eagerly watching these things happen."

Wow, what is coming for us?

The Hope of The Party

I had to ask that question, surprisingly enough, when a party we were hosting at our home was cruelly interrupted.

It was a little early to light candles. I looked around the room and enjoyed the muted afternoon sunlight coming through the French doors. I liked it. There was a familiar comfort, this moment a few hours before a large group of dinner guests arrived to celebrate Christmas. I was happy with the clean hardwood floors. That could seem shallow, perhaps, except that I love preparing for guests. I smelled the subtle scent of pine and spied the bags and candles for the luminarias near the front door, ready to be assembled. I imagined the white lights on the Christmas tree at dusk, no longer hidden by daylight. There was still much to do, but in this moment I stopped to envision each person around the table, discovering and enjoying each other. A group of gold was coming to our home—funny, authentic, thoughtful, selfless folks. All so different. I couldn't wait to see them.

I had been preparing food for days. I felt like Babette in *Babette's Feast*, without the lottery. Visions of each course had rumbled around in my head, found their way into the freezer, and then near the oven on this day. I enjoyed every moment. I had been weary going into the holidays, a calendar heavy with events. But this feast was going to be the final act before a nice long intermission over Christmas. And we had much to celebrate.

I moved toward the serving cabinet to get utensils when I noticed I had missed a call. I placed the cutlery at the place settings and wandered to the phone. My sister had called.

What is it that tells the heart all is not well, the intuition, the knowing? It was the Spirit of Jesus. Be prepared. I listened to my sister's rended voice on a message, and I knew. I called and she quickly picked up, crying as I've never heard: "Ryan is dead."

The words tumbled like an avalanche of heavy stone into my center, crushing it. My nephew Ryan's face, his essence, was immediately before the eyes of my spirit, scenes from his life flickering past in rapid succession, landing on a walk I had with him by the Rio Grande in warm winter sun just three weeks prior. I envisioned my sister's eyes, and I crumpled to the floor.

I will not describe the words pouring from my sister's heart. They are sacred words, words of passionate affection, longing, and knowledge of her son. They cascaded from a heart shattered like glass. And I cannot describe the words that rose up in me to meet her words. Our cry rose to heaven, with him.

The party, the feast, the preparation, the pleasure, vanished into a fog. The room was swallowed up in shock. The warming oven, the bubbling cider, stopped. It did not dare move. Ryan was gone, and the rest of the world went silent.

The next nine hours were a heightened blur. Calls to cancel the party. Hurried packing. A call to our brother. A call to arrange care for the dogs. Steve and I drove south to New Mexico in the dark. Friends derailed from the party gathered instead to pray for my heartbroken family and called along the way. The miles were like molasses, and we crawled through a high desert blizzard.

Ryan's face was all I could see. I saw his wry three year-old face, certain even then of his attire, down to his choice of socks. I saw the slight tilt of his head, as his twenty-five year-old penetrating gaze quietly inquired of me, curious about Steve's software, my counseling work, our family. I felt his creative soul, saw his paintings, heard his writing. I saw the familiar, familial pain deep in his eyes, the cost of bearing a sensitive spirit in a harsh world. I saw his glimmering smile. How handsome.

We arrived. What I saw in the eyes of those I love can't be articulated. It is something I never want to see again, looks not intended for this world.

It is my sister's to tell, and human words are paltry, but in the middle of it all she was given a vision. Not a wish, not a fantasy, not something she created—but a vision. It was a mother's knowledge, yes, but much more than that. Jesus brought to her an understanding, a sight, into what Ryan now is, what he knows, what he's *doing*. I wish that every human being could watch her eyes as she tells of it, the excitement, the joy, the *pride*. She saw Ryan, fully creative, his artistry and brilliance pouring from him, unabated. He is having so much fun. He is delighted at what he is accomplishing. Nothing is blocking him. He's Ryan, fully, finally, Ryan.

Death does nothing but take. It removed the warmth of Ryan's body, his strong, athletic arms, his scent. It removed the ability to touch him, hold him, to see clearly his eyes. It took his parent's dreams of their son's career, life with God, the beautiful children he would bring into this world. Death interrupts and attempts to mock, tries to proclaim itself king. It is horrible in all its collateral damage.

But it does not get to have a final sting.

Some of the most beautiful words ever penned came from Paul, whose life had been completely changed by Jesus. He once hated Christians, killed them. But he became the man who said, "Death is swallowed up in victory. O Death, where is your victory? O Death, where is your sting?" He's not talking about some religious victory, some moral high ground. And he's not talking about some ethereal cloud of disembodied spirits, rallying around the throne of God, like floating cherubs on clouds. No, the reality is "our bodies are buried in brokenness, but will be raised in glory. Our bodies will be transformed." When you hear the term "good news," think mostly about the force that destroys death, that will renew us, deliver us into a new heaven, a new earth, a great party, a feast, one full of faces we've longed to be with, the warmth of hearth, fantastic wine, delicious food, the best dancing music, unencumbered by any hint of shame or shadow.

All of those things that keep us muted, covered over, slightly blocked, will be gone, and we can enjoy being ourselves.

In fact, that is what Jesus is most excited about: "Look, God's home is now among his people! He will live with them and they will be his people. God himself will be with them. He will wipe every tear from their eyes, and there will be no more death or sorrow or crying or pain. All these things are gone forever. Look, I am making everything new" (Rev. 21:4-6)!

We will, *finally*, be his people. We will be who we were intended to be. Buechner says, "Maybe the process of giving birth to a human is what is happening at all times, if we let it. We are becoming more of ourselves, because in 'that day' we get to be fully ourselves." In that day you will be the same comic you've always been, only funnier. Maybe you'll be the peaceful, contemplative one—you'll have that in spades. Perhaps you are the fiery presence in the room, and you'll feel the full freedom of flames coming from your passionate heart. Maybe you like to ride elephants. Well, the elephants will come when you beckon them. It will be God's delight to bring to you whatever will make you more at home, more of yourself. The one who created, redeemed, and restored you did not bring you to this kingdom in order to mass-produce a choir around the throne. The music will contain *your* song.

And we'll see Jesus as he really is. Finally, we'll see the one we were getting to know, to varying degrees, the one we suspected was real midst the ridiculous counterfeit renderings of him. It will be his land, after all. He rules it and proclaims that we get to be ourselves, finally ourselves.

I want to ride horses with him, thanking him for keeping my heart alive through all the times I wanted to despair. And I want to play with children. A young woman I know wants to talk to him a long time, giving him a chance to explain some things to her. I think of myriad girls and boys enslaved in the sex trade who will, for the first time, be able to even think about what they want. We'll be so glad that we were restored and made new that we won't think about worship. We'll worship by being ourselves.

We drove back north to Colorado, to our house, too soon it seemed. The place settings were still on the table, the cider on the stove, food thrown haphazardly in the freezer. There were remnants everywhere of an intended party.

And that's where we find ourselves. Waiting for the party to be restored. All good parties point to it, give us an idea of it. Ryan's there. Mom and my brother Dick are there. Brent, Jim, and Mark are there. I can't wait to see how my mom is helping Jesus tell people who they really are with her sparkling eyes. I can't wait to see my brother Dick exploring the mountains and making people laugh. My friend Brent is enjoying the best cigar and fishing the sweetest river. Saint Augustine said that there "[w]e shall rest and see, see and love . . . . For what other end do we propose to ourselves than to attain the kingdom for which there is no end?"[28]

I can't wait to see what Ryan has been working on. I can't wait to see the pleasure in Jesus' eyes as he invites his boy to show him, and us, his latest creation, something that, as his dad says, would make the flowers sing. I don't imagine Ryan surrounded by clouds and sleepy peace. I prefer how Dallas Willard describes it: "peace as wholeness, as fullness of function, as the restful but unending creativity involved in a cosmos-wide, cooperative pursuit of a created order that continuously approaches but never reaches the limitless and greatness of the triune personality of God, its source."[29] Yes, Ryan is busy.

He's having a blast, and I want him to show me what he's created for, and with, Jesus.

What a great thing to do before sitting down for some really good food.

Beauty Trumps Bitch

Your heart aches for that place! Buechner says, "Our very brokenness here speaks of wholeness and holiness. The emptiness we carry around inside us through the dust whispers like a seashell of the great sea that it belongs to and that belongs to it."[30] There are lots of owls there, and definitely no loss of babies. Finally, there will be no veneer of falsehood, no hiding. No bitch.

At his last meal with his friends, Jesus said, "So you have sorrow now, but I will see you again and your hearts will rejoice, and no one will take your joy from you. In that day you ask nothing of me. Truly, truly I say to you if you ask anything of the Father, he will give it to you in my name." So let's ask him to help us to let go of our control, let go of our pride, and let go of our addictions—even in this long wait of the meantime. He knows the end of the story, and when we taste what kind of beauty awaits us, what kind of beauty we will finally be, all of our foolishness will seem so, well, foolish.

Remember the mug I threw? You wouldn't be able to discern it if you came to our home, but I have left a little bit of that splattered milk on the wall. It is a monument of sorts, an Ebenezer, my pile of stones, to the impact of a hard heart. It is a monument to pride, to the contempt that rises as I try to justify myself. But it is far more a monument to a God who mocks my independence of him with a wink. When I get there, it will be a monument to love.

One of the greatest gifts I was ever given was from a young woman who knew degradation from the hands of those who were meant to shelter and shepherd her, and who has bludgeoned herself in a crucible of her own sexual addiction. She knows the humiliation that comes from the screeching glee of demons. It was impossible to hear her tell the things done to her without tasting the sorrow of God. And it was impossible to see her take responsibility for the destructive things she had chosen in response to her pain without tasting the grace of God. It was a joy to sit with her, to hear of her life, because the inextinguishable light in her eyes was tenacious, always wanting to come out of hiding.

She is an artist, and her precision with words astounded me. Her ability to capture her inner world and the world she witnessed often made me envious. My hesitancy to share with you the gift she gave me is washed over with the desire for you to imagine the triune sweetness, the truth and goodness and beauty, of the moment she read this to me:

> *For Jan*
> *the sound of your laughter rips down*
> *bulky drapes*
> *flings open doors to light-starved rooms*
> *hammers open jammed windows*

lets sour air out
something goes free
knots untie themselves
darkness scurries from corners, shamed

It says, "I was once pressed down and
couldn't breathe."
you laugh
old ropes fly apart
bursting into waves of confetti
faith can be heard
in the laughter of free women
they laugh, "Surely God has
helped us up to this point."

Nothing could have floored me more. Hearing her words felt like a homecoming, a moment of relief that someone's eyes have seen what I hoped was true but never fathomed could be in the midst of my own war with the bitch inside of me. She could not have known the dark war of shame raging in my own heart, even the day on which she read it. She did not know that I sometimes I throw mugs, tear down my husband's dignity, disassociate through rituals of control, pout, complain, sneer, and withhold! But she was right, and gratitude won, and I sat in silent honor of the blood I have shed to know the freedom she named. I am free. I am in an ongoing war with my own self-contempt, but I am growing in freedom every day.

With each season I am discovering that the bitch, she's just not needed anymore. And this, more than any other thing, is a sought-after, fought-for, but completely surprising gift.

Faith can be heard in the laughter of free women. Beauty seeps unexpectedly from hearts that have given themselves over to the power of love. Goodness, Truth and Beauty blend and flow from those who have a sober sense of how ridiculous it is that women such as ourselves—prideful, fearful, controlling, raging, addicted women—might have a burst of confetti, a spark of life.

---

[26] My thanks to Rev. Joel Pinson for this image.

[27] Frederick Buechner, *A Room Called Remember* (New York: HarperCollins, 1984), 103.

[28] St. Augustine, *The City of God*, book 19, paragraph 17.

[29] Dallas Willard, *The Divine Conspiracy: Rediscovering our Hidden Life in God* (San Francisco: Harper San Francisco, 1988), 400.

[30] Buechner, 103.

Acknowledgements

How any message gets crafted into someone's heart is a mysterious blend of history, topography, people, wounding, joy, healing, boredom, grace, forgiveness, and an eventual emerging from the collision of those things with a sense of release and freedom – and gratitude. My father Walt Meyers and my mother Mary Meyers (who has been enjoying the fruits of the kingdom for a few years now) have known a life few of us can imagine as Depression and WWII era folks who understand what it is to suffer, and to delight in simple things. Mom and dad also lived a tenacious loyalty and fidelity midst a crucible of a life together. The stories shared on these pages are done so with the deepest gratitude for the comprehensive beauty of their lives.

I thank those whose stories are reflected here, with anonymity intact, for changing me with your lives. And I thank Patton Dodd, publisher extraordinaire, for his keen eyes, kind hand and his belief in this project.

I love my husband Steve more than life. I'm grateful for your kind and patient strength, my love— and your courage to bless a book such as this. You are a man among men.

And I thank Jesus for being beautiful – always.

About the Author

Jan Meyers Proett has been a counselor for over twenty years and is the author of *The Allure of Hope* and *Listening to Love*. She has worked on behalf of exploited women internationally, but also loves the trails of Colorado, where she lives with her husband, Steve. Follow Jan at her Facebook page (http://www.facebook.com/janproett) and her blog (http://www.janmeyersproett.com/).

If you enjoyed *Beauty and the Bitch*, head over to Amazon, write a review, and check out other works by Jan Meyers Proett.

About Bondfire Books

Bondfire Books is an independent epublisher based in Colorado and New York City. We publish fiction and nonfiction—both originals and back-list titles—by today's top writing talent, from established voices to up-and-comers. Learn more about Bondfire and our complete list of titles at www.bondfirebooks.com. Follow us on Twitter @bondfirebooks and find us on Facebook at facebook.com/bondfirebooks.